Technical Analysis
in the
Options
Market

WILEY FINANCE EDITIONS

Technical Analysis

in the
Options
Market

*The Effective Use
of Computerized
Trading Systems*

Richard Hexton

John Wiley & Sons, Inc.
New York ▲ Chichester ▲ Brisbane ▲ Toronto ▲ Singapore

Copyright © 1990, 1993, 1995 by Richard Hexton
Published by John Wiley & Sons, Inc.

Library of Congress Cataloging-in-Publication Data:

Hexton, Richard
  Technical Analysis in the
  Options Market/Richard Hexton
  p. cm.
  Includes index
  ISBN 0-471-08489-1
Printed in the United States of America

10 9 8 7 6 5 4 3 2 1

Contents

Preface

The aim of this book is to highlight the computerized programs and charting techniques that I personally have found most useful and profitable when trading the options market.

One of the main objectives of computerized technical analysis programs is to develop a system that not only identifies market trends correctly but also produces consistently good results. 'Easier said than done!' you may well reply. However, this book does not suggest that the techniques and systems identified are in any way unique. It does show that by careful understanding of the markets and by filtering out the more successful products and charting techniques that I personally have found very profitable, it is possible for the serious trader to save many laborious hours of having to test systems and analyse charting methods. More importantly, he or she will benefit from enhanced trading systems.

This book not only highlights successes that have been achieved using the more traditional methods of charting but also includes an in-depth study of the latest acceptable techniques of Japanese chart patterns known as candlesticks charts. These two chapters alone make the book a must for the serious trader.

Richard Hexton

1

The Psychology of Success

I often read about 'the psychology of investment' rather than 'the psychology of success'. Indeed, the opening chapter of my previous book about options was entitled 'The psycholoy of investment'. But surely what we are all trying to achieve is success. Consequently, I thought it would be more appropriate, this time around, to commence the revised edition of 'Technical Analysis in the Options Market' with a discussion of the psychology related to achieving success.

This book will be concentrating on the techniques of technical analysis; but it is also important to understand the psychology of disciplined trading and the rules and procedures that need to be adhered to in order to continue to succeed in the market-place. It is not easy! Simulated trading is a far cry from trading the real market.

So what is this magic word 'success'? It is all very well to make bland statements such as 'Stop dreaming and start succeeding', but how does one set out on the path to success? First of all it is important not to let opportunities pass you by. The reason why the rich and successful are rich and successful is that they seized on the opportunities that other people had thought were too good to be true.

You may think this is a far cry from technical analysis, but ask yourself, 'Why am I studying technical analysis?' In most cases the answer must be to maximize your returns in the market-place, and this can be achieved by timing your entry and exit points with the aid of technical analysis. This maximization of your returns will, in turn, lead to your success; but only if you understand yourself and adhere to the necessary disciplines and procedures.

This message of psychology and disciplined trading will be repeated many times throughout the early part of this book, because I know how easy it is to become emotionally involved in the market, believing you have the perfect system (which may well be true) only to find out that you don't adhere to its rules once you have put your toe in the water and begun trading. Later on, I will highlight the methods that I have used to overcome these emotions of fear and greed.

Success in the market can be attributed to two main factors: first, psychology and, secondly, trading techniques. However, 90 per cent of this success can be attributed to psychology. With the right trading techniques and the wrong psychology, I can almost guarantee that however good your trading system appears, you will still fail to achieve the success you desire in the market-place. Hopefully, by the time you have read this book, not only will you have learnt some important aspects of technical analysis, but you will be able to apply these techniques in the real market with considerable success. Simply put, in most cases your attitudes must and will have changed. Although this might sound very patronising, in order to achieve a high rate of continued success, then it is imperative to have the right state if mind. It is also important to think positively and not negatively. It is not what happens to you that matters, but how you react to it.

STAYING THE COURSE AND KNOWING WHEN TO GET OUT

It is one thing to sense the possibility of success. It is quite another to have the courage and faith to trade – to 'stay the course'. The old saying remains true: 'It is no use giving a man a gun, if he doesn't have the courage to pull the trigger'. Most investors, having committed their financial shirt, run for cover at the first opportunity – so, this is where the concept of disciplined trading must be obeyed. If you are not sure whether this is possible, then commence trading with perhaps only one contract and endeavour to obey the rules implicitly. Even if you lose money on this first trade, at least you will have the satisfaction of knowing that you did adhere to all the rules and it may now be necessary to adapt your trading system for future trades.

The other requirement is knowing when to get out. It should already have been decided when to exit from a trade before you commence trading. The exit point may be triggered by a simple stop-loss or stop-profit system or, perhaps, by a more complex filter or moving-average system; but all these rules should be in place before you enter into the trade and – more importantly – you yourself must be aware of these rules. If necessary, highlight the important rules by writing them down.

A successful trader must of course be familiar with market rules and the rules of his or her own trading strategy; but there is much more to it than that. Even superior knowledge will not necessarily make a successful trader. The essential quality of the successful trader is that he or she must employ a superior strategy which, with the acquired knowledge, will result in a tally of more correct decisions than is achieved by opponents or competitors. Also, wrong decisions should be cut as soon as possible with minimal losses while, in turn, allowing profits to run.

WHAT IS A STRATEGY?

A strategy is a planned method of achieving an objective – and the better the strategy the greater the chance one has of achieving that objective.

Of course, each person will adopt their own strategy with different objectives in mind. One trader might have a strategy that is geared towards intra-day trading and hence the objectives will clearly be different from another trader who is looking to position trade over a longer period with possible higher stop-losses than those of the intra-day trader: in turn, the latter's objectives will be longer term than the intra-day trader. Each trader must adopt a strategy that suits their own individual personality and, before adopting such a suitable strategy, it will also be necessary to make some basic assessments about yourself and what factors and influences could affect the outcome of your decisions. Above all, the strategy must give you the confidence to trade the market successfully and to adhere to the adopted strategy system.

I know everyone is looking for that perfect strategy – but, believe me, it does not exist. There are going to be times when the market does not work in favour of your system and you must accept this. Not every trade is going to be correct: but by understanding beforehand that losses will inevitably occur, then you will certainly be starting on the road to success. The trader who cannot accept losses and believes that a system will be correct every time will not succeed in the market-place.

Once you have tested your system over a number of years (or whatever period you consider to be suitable for the type of trading you propose to adopt), then stick to it! Don't change the rules the very first time that the trade results in a loss. The next trade will probably be missed either because you are too busy changing your rules and/or the new rule change adopted misses out the next trade and this would have been the very one under the old rules that would have been profitable. I am not saying the system cannot be enhanced, but this is exactly what the changes should be – minor enhancements and not a fundamental alteration to the trading strategy. The major rules for the system should still be in place.

MAJOR AND MINOR TRADING RULES

I have found that the trading rules that suit my personality involve the following criteria. First, I have a 'major rule' which signals either a 'major sell' or a 'major buy' in the market-place. Once this signal is activated then I have secondary or 'minor rules' which provide signals that are used to pyramid the trade (as long as the major rule is still in place). In this way you will be maximizing your returns in a trending market, whereas in a non-trending, sideways market the secondary signals will not be activated.

The result is that in a non-trending market the major rule is often closed out with a small profit or in some cases a small loss and the secondary, minor signals are not generated, so no further trades are activated. In a strongly trending market, on the other hand, the system allows the profits to run and also to pyramid up the market, resulting in further increased profits. It all sounds very easy, but of course it all comes back to the same old problem – finding and adopting a suitable trading strategy and then adhering to the rules!

Signals on the FTSE

Charts 1.1–1.3 highlight the major and secondary signals for the FTSE 100 Index I have adopted, and that have been activated by the system over the past three years. (For further back data and information on the RH Technical Analysis Trending System, please write to Richard Hexton, Suite C, 6 Cromwell Crescent, London SW5 9QN.

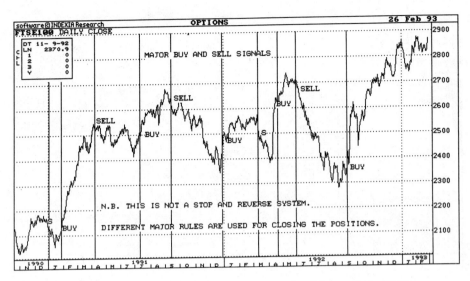

Chart 1.1   FTSE 100 daily close, major signals, November 1990–February 1993

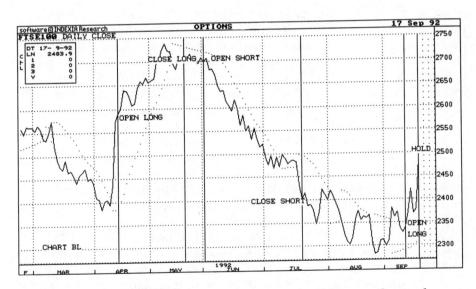

Chart 1.2   FTSE 100 daily close, major signals, February–September 1992

Chart 1.1 highlights the *major* buy and sell signals for the FTSE 100 daily close for the period November 1990–February 1993. As mentioned on the chart, this is not a stop and reverse system: it highlights the *opening*

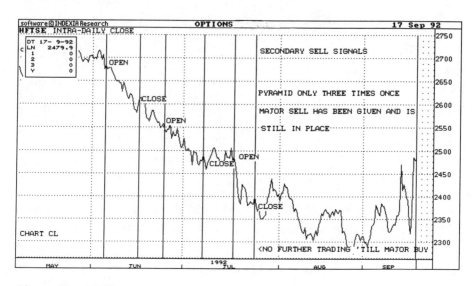

Chart 1.3   FTSE 100 intra-daily close, secondary signals,
May–September 1992

positions for going long or short, and the chart merely illustrates that
these are the major rules to open a position in the market. As long as the
major long rule is still in place, then secondary long rules can be applied
for pyramiding and, similarly, with the short signals as well. For instance,
a major sell on the FTSE 100 was given on 16 July 1990 at 2406 and, more
recently, on 1 June 1992 at 2697. A major buy signal was generated on 30
December 1991 at 2420 and on 10 September 1992 at 2413.

Chart 1.2 is a zoomed version of Chart 1.1, highlighting the *closing*
major positions for the FTSE 100 during the period February to September
1992. A major buy was given on 13 April 1992 at 2591 and the major
closing position was triggered on 20 May 1992 at 2711 (a gain of 120
points). Then, a major sell signal was triggered by the system on 1 June
1992 at 2697 and this in turn was closed out by the major closing signal on
20 July 1992 at 2377 (a gain of 320 points).

Chart 1.3 highlights the *secondary* buy and sell signals for the FTSE 100
Index. In fact, the secondary signals are based on three inputs at different
times during the course of the day (further explanation concerning these
inputs is included later on in the book). The principle is that secondary
signals will only be applied in the direction of the market and as long as
the major signal is still in place. – ie, if a major buy signal has been
activated then only secondary buy signals would be generated. At no time
would the system be recommending short positions while a major long
(buy) signal was in place. As long as the major buy is still in place then a
long secondary signal can be activated, and vice versa for a sell signal.

In summary, once you have understood the technical aspects of your computerized system, then the next most important step is to adopt and adhere to a successful trading strategy. Perhaps the best suggestion I can make with regards to this latter rule of adherence is that on commencement you should 'undertrade' – in other words, just trade one contract at at time until you are confident that you can and will stick to the rules. Excessive overtrading will be too onerous at commencement (especially if the first trade goes wrong), and you will then undoubtedly start to change the technical analysis system that you have so patiently built up. Clearly, if you can stay with your winning trades and cut your losses by simply obeying the rules, then you have the potential of a profitable portfolio!

The purpose of this first chapter has been to outline the techniques of trading that I use in the market-place. Certainly, at the beginning of a bull market it is easier and more profitable to run with the tide. But it is the successful investor who can identify the final stages of this cycle and it is the art of astute timing that then becomes of paramount importance. However, to come out of the market near its peak is easier said than done! The same is true at the other extreme – ie, to invest in the market when it has been declining for some time and when one tends to believe that the decline is unstoppable. Timing is one of the most important concepts in the traded options market and we will be studying in more detail (particularly in Chapter 4) the short-term oscillators that assist greatly in this area.

2

Trend Recognition

I am sure most of you have heard of the old adages 'The trend is your friend' and 'Don't buck the trend', but finding your friend and retaining that friendship isn't always so easy. Of course there is plenty of advice out there from so-called professionals on where they believe the market is heading and inviting you to climb aboard their band-wagon – only to find out that a false alarm had been triggered and you have to get off at the very next stop.

It always reminds me of a couple of paintings in my sister's house. The first painting depicts a Victorian horse and carriage with the driver seated: approaching a cliff's edge, the horse starts to bolt. The caption underneath says 'Time to jump out!'. The next painting depicts the carriage going over the cliff top and the caption under this painting says 'Too late to climb out!' This is all rather similar to many opportunities made and lost in the market. Unlike most traders, the successful trader aims to climb aboard an existing trend once this new trend has been confirmed by his or her technical indicators. Then, not only is it important to remain with the trend but to seek opportunities to maximize returns by pyramiding while the trend is still in existence.

NEW TRENDS AND THEIR DEVELOPMENT

The questions that arise, therefore, are 'How long is this trend?' and 'How long should I stick with it?' The first question must be answered by referring back to your objectives. Obviously a position trader will be studying longer-term trends than will be an intra-day trader, so technical indicators will need to be adjusted accordingly. Whereas a four-hourly trend might be in existence for an intra-day trader, a four-week trend might be more appropriate for the position trader. No matter what your objectives are, however, you must stick with the trend all the time until your technical indicators confirm that it has been broken.

For example, on the sterling/dollar chart which follows, my technical indicators confirmed that a new uptrend had come into existence for sterling on 23 April 1992 at 17645 and that this uptrend continued to exist until 15 September 1992, when a new downtrend was heralded (see Chart 2.1). At this time I did not know that the new downtrend would be so explosive and rapid. But the point is that significant profits were made by pyramiding the uptrend of the sterling/dollar spot market between the months of April and August. Again, a major buy signal was the first indicator of the new uptrend and secondary, minor buy signals were used to pyramid this uptrend as long as the major buy was still in existence.

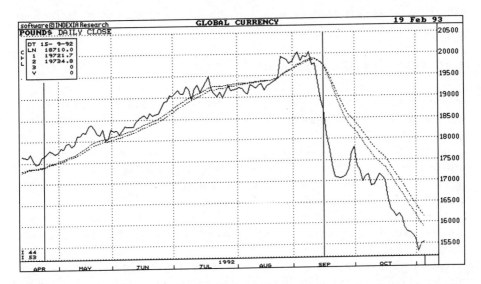

Chart 2.1 Sterling/dollar chart shows a new uptrend and a new downtrend

Similarily with the FTSE 100 Index – there was a clear downtrend in existence from the beginning of June 1992 until the end of August (see Chart 1.2). Of course, I am not saying that you will be able to identify these trends at their commencement and/or exit them at their conclusion. But, by careful use of your indicators, you should be able to confirm the end of an uptrend and identify the beginning of a new downtrend. The trend may only last for a couple of weeks or, in the case of the FTSE 100, three months. However, I can almost guarantee that when the new trend is signalled, whether it be the beginning of a new uptrend from a previous devastating downtrend or vice versa, the trader rarely believes his indicators and, to make matters worse, usually fails to activate a trade.

After many weeks of hard work and testing the system through simulated trading, the day arrives when you are in a position to trade and the signal is finally generated, but you fail to pull the trigger on your gun! You begin to make excuses for not trading, such as: 'Yes! We were due a technical rally and, since the market is now so overbought, I will wait for the overbought indicator to unwind itself.' Inevitably the market continues to climb and (excuse number two) you now think it is too late to enter. Another possibility is that the technical analyst decides to enter into the realms of fundamentals, looking for any excuse to prevent trading taking place: 'Surely it is not possible for this market to rally when the recession is still biting so hard?' Or: 'anyway, interest rates will now have to rise to protect against further declines in sterling!' But again the analyst fails to activate any trades, although the technical indicators are still in place and shouting at the trader to go long of the market!

Understanding the system and yourself

When the signal generated finally proves to be correct and the market has moved away, you now try and justify the reasons for not having traded: 'This trade would have been too risky anyway and the risk/reward ratio in these volatile markets was too high.' Or: 'Yes! It was more prudent to stay out of this trade, since the downside potential was far greater than the possible upside' (even though the market had already fallen over 300 points). 'I'll wait for the next signal and will definitely trade then, come hell or high water!' Of course you fail to realise or appreciate that if you had followed this signal, you would now be sitting on a handsome profit, with 200 plus points behind you!

You've guessed it. The next signal comes along and you actually trade it this time. But it proves to be the very signal that goes wrong and you close the position with a loss. You feel dejected and decide to call it a day, leaving the market to the so-called professionals in the belief that your system has let you down. This could not be further from the truth. All that has happened is that you have only traded once and the previous trade you missed out on would have in fact made you a handsome profit and probably the next trade as well. It is your self-discipline, lack of trust in the system and your failure to understand yourself and your strategy that has led to your current predicament. Let's now see how to recognise a *trend* in the real market and what methods we can hope to adopt in order to stick with that trend.

One additional important point to mention at this stage is that as a trend develops it tends to pick up momentum, feeding on its own strengths or weaknesses. We will study the momentum indicator in Chapter 4 and see its relationship to a trend. Finally, before going on to the charts, I should mention another important indicator that can be used to confirm a trend – the directional movement indicator. This indicator will be discussed in detail in this chapter, complete with charts and worked examples.

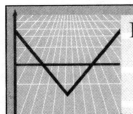
TREND LINES

Trend lines are constructed when a chosen market price has bounced off a particular line three or more times. Some analysts only use any two high or any two low points to construct such a trend; but these could be unreliable. I personally prefer to see at least three points of connection – the theory being that the more times the market bounces off the line before penetrating it the more reliable it will be. A trend line is broken when the market price level closes below the trend line of rising troughs in a bull market, or rises up through a trend line of successive peaks in a falling market.

In this chapter we will also be studying the use of speed lines and Fibonacci fan lines, together with worked examples of parallel trend lines and trend channels. Initially, it may be appropriate to illustrate some point and figure charts with a 45 degree trend line overlaid.

Point and figure charts

Point and figure charts facilitate the study of pure price movement. In other words, when plotting a point and figure chart, there is no consideration for the time element and only price changes are recorded on the chart.

Two columns appear on a point and figure chart: A series of 'X's and series of '0's. As long as the price progression continues in one direction, the 'X's are placed in a single column, one above the other, as in the case of an upward move. When there is a change of direction (reversal), the '0' is placed in the next column to the right.

There are two ways to vary a point and figure chart:

1.   Change the value of the box (X or 0).
2.   Change the reversal criteria. This would be the number of boxes needed to generate a reversal.

Thus a point and figure chart can be made either more sensitive by using a smaller criteria for the box size and/or the reversal requirement, or less sensitive by using a larger box size and/or a larger reversal requirement.

The 45 degree support line

Because of the severe condensation of point and figure charts, it would not be practical to try and join up the rally tops or reaction lows. The 45 degree line is, therefore, used.

In an uptrend, the bullish support line is drawn at a 45 degree angle upward to the right from under the last column of '0's. As long as the prices remain above that line, the major trend is considered to be bullish. In a downtrend, the bearish resistance line is drawn at a 45 degree angle downward to the right from the top of the highest column of 'X's. As long as prices remain below that trend line, the trend is bearish.

Occasionally, these 45 degree lines have to be adjusted. For instance, if the major resistance line is broken on the upside for a brief period; but also if the price drops below it again to recommend the downtrend. In this case a new 45 degree line would be drawn from the top of the last reaction.

The point and figure charts for Marks and Spencer and Boots (Charts 2.2 and 2.3 clearly illustrate the 45 degree support line continuing to act as a support level.

TRENDS

A trend is often a steady and reliable pattern that enables the investor to build up a certain amount of confidence in his ability to trade in the market. Basically, there are two types of trends:

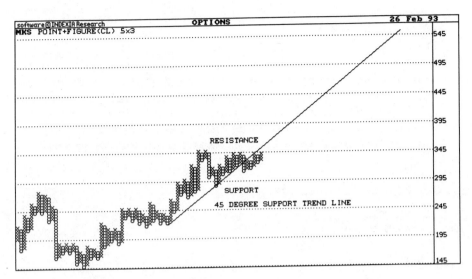

Chart 2.2 Marks and Spencer point and figure

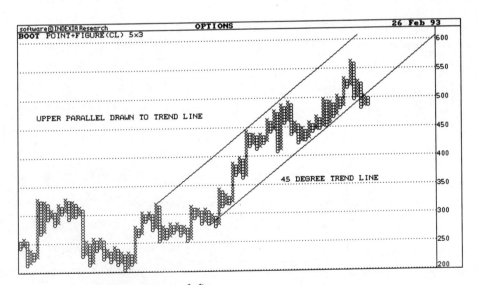

Chart 2.3 Boots point and figure

1. **Uptrend**

   In order for an uptrend to exist, it is necessary to connect the lower points of the share price during its rise. For confirmation of an uptrend, analysts like to see contact of at least three points before it is considered to be valid. The longer the trend line has been in force, the more validity it will have.

2. **Downtrend**

As the name implies, a downtrend is the exact opposite of the uptrend. However, here we are connecting the top points of the share prices or indices which, when joined together, form a downtrend.

Whereas the uptrend gives support to the share price, in the downtrend, the share price finds resistance and each time the share price reaches this level it bounces away from it to a lower level.

Uptrends and downtrends

Medium-term trends

Chart 2.4 clearly shows the medium-term uptrend for British Airways remaining intact from August 1991 to June 1992. There were four points of contact, followed by penetration of the uptrend initially occurring at the end of June and, finally, a clear break down at the end of July.

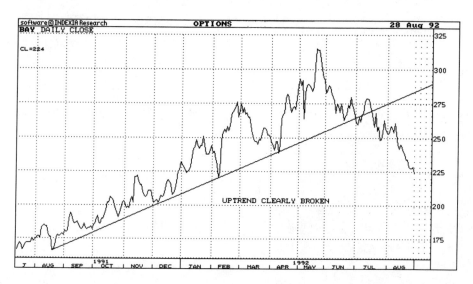

Chart 2.4   British Airways daily close, July 1991–August 1992

In order to confirm that the uptrend line has finally been broken, I find it useful to use 'INDEXIA filters' as a confirmatory signal. If the trend line has been broken and the filters are also stating a sell signal, then

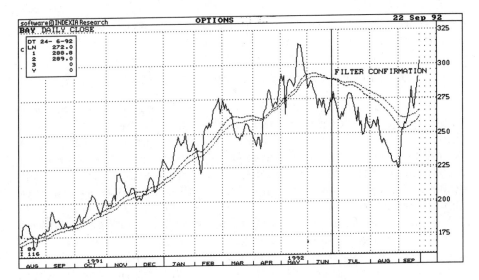

OPTIONS

22 Sep 92

software@INDEXIA Research

BAY DAILY CLOSE

```
DT 24- 6-92
LN    272.0
1     288.8
2     289.0
3       0
Y       0
```

FILTER CONFIRMATION

325

300

275

250

225

200

175

1989
I 116

AUG | SEP | OCT | NOV | DEC | JAN | FEB | MAR | APR | MAY | JUN | JUL | AUG | SEP

1991   1992

Chart 2.5 British Airways daily close – filter confirmation

appropriate action should be taken. The previous chart confirmed the uptrend had been broken and, with the use of the INDEXIA filters, a sell of the stock can be confirmed (see Chart 2.5). As at the end of June the uptrend had been broken and on 24 June the filters were also confirming a sell; therefore, without any further assistance from other technical indicators, the strategy would have been either to sell the stock or perhaps to purchase put options or write call options against the stock.

Indexia filters

The 'Indexia filters' use a proprietary formula for their calculation. They use adaptive filtering techniques and hence adjust the weights according to the movement of the figures.

The filters are similar to moving averages, but are far more efficient. They also follow the price action very closely and give a much earlier trading signal both in and out of the market when compared to moving averages.

The share price did in fact fall approximately 50p (or 18 per cent) from these levels. One can therefore start to build up a picture as to when to buy stock and when to sell or protect it. At this stage we have only just touched on the simple aspects of trend formation and the INDEXIA filters. Also, please note that these filters can be optimized to suit the type of trading you wish to execute. In the previous example I have illustrated a medium-term analytical approach. For a shorter-term approach, you need to optimize the filters over a shorter period and also look at shorter-term trends, and vice versa for longer-term trends.

Purchasing put options and writing call options

As this book is also aimed at non-professional investors, I thought it would be prudent to give a brief insight into how the traded options market works in relation to the purchase of 'put' options and the use of 'covered call writing'. Both of these strategies can be used as a source of protection. Purchasing put options is the opposite to purchasing 'call' options. Put options allow the investor to 'sell' shares at an agreed price (ie to *put* them onto a new owner).

The purchase of put options is used to take advantage of a downward market or share movement. In general, a decrease in the price of a share results in an increase in the price of a put option's premium. A call option is purchased when one is optimistic about the future price rise of a share or indices, whereas a put option is purchased when one is pessimistic about the share price or indices (ie you believe that they are going to fall).

For the serious investor, the skilful use of put options clearly increases the number of strategies open to him. As a decrease in the market price of the share can subsequently result in an increase in the premium of a put option, it can be sold or exercised at a profit. A clear understanding of this reverse arithmetic is absolutely essential to an understanding of put options and their uses.

Both the amount and speed of any fall in the price of an underlying share will have an effect on premium prices. Understanding the importance of timing and its effect on premium prices will prove a vital part of your success in the traded options market.

A put option whose exercise price is above the current market price of the underlying security is said to be 'in the money'; whereas a put option whose exercise price is below the current price of the underlying security is said to be 'out of the money'. When the share price and the exercise price are the same, the option is said to be 'at the Money'.

Writing options

'Selling' or 'writing' trade options represents the other side of the coin in the options market. The writing of options plays a very important role. Whereas the buyer of a traded option pays a premium, a writer (seller) of a traded option receives a premium. However, in return for receiving a premium, the writer of an option incurs a liability. In the case of a call option he is obligated to supply those shares to a holder of a call option who has exercised his right on the option contract. In the case of a put option, the investor who has written a put option incurs the liability to purchase the underlying stock at the exercise price chosen at any time until expiry.

Covered call writing

Covered call writing implies that you already own the shares and are willing to give them up for a guaranteed maximum sale price.

So, when writing options, 'time value' is to your advantage. As time evaporates, so the premium reduces, and the buy back premium option is cheaper, thus leaving you with a net profit. Remember when writing options, time works in your favour; but when buying options, time works against you.

Another factor to take into consideration, is your expectations of the share price movement. Are you neutral, bearish or bullish? Your expectations will determine which exercise price you select. Most writers tend to opt for 'out of the money' options, and your view of the share price movement will determine how deep an out of the money exercise price you select.

To summarise, covered call writing is a form of protection and is a conservative strategy. A covered writer of a call option is one who owns the underlying security. He is known as 'covered' because, if the option is exercised, he will have to sell the security at the exercise price and he is able to do so from his existing holdings, rather than having to go into the market to buy it first. If he deposits the actual share underlying the option contract as collateral, rather than other forms of margin, then this is known as 'cover'.

Optimised filters and moving averages

This is a relatively new program introduced by Indexia. It is designed for making profits using moving averages and Indexia's filters.

Moving averages, when used correctly, are one of the most powerful tools available to the technical analyst. Unfortunately, the decision as to how many averages, what type and especially what periods to use, makes moving average analysis really quite difficult – even for the professional.

Indexia's moving average manager program literally takes all the guess work out of the analysis with moving averages. It enables the analyst to determine not only the best type of average to use, but also the best periods. It is able to store the results, so that they can be used to tell you which of the files in your databank are in 'buy' and 'sell' modes and how long they have been in that mode, based on the optimised averages.

The program produces an historic trade summary for any share, or any other data file, so that you can see exactly where and when signals were given as well as the profit on each trade, including dealing costs, if you wish.

Short- and long-term trends

Chart 2.6 for Kingfisher clearly illustrates a short-term downtrend formation in existence from June 1992 to August 1992. The downtrend was eventually broken at point B in the middle of August and, although the share price did come back initially, a new, dramatic upward movement followed. The downtrend was no longer in existence, and one should have been put on notice that there was more potential for the upside.

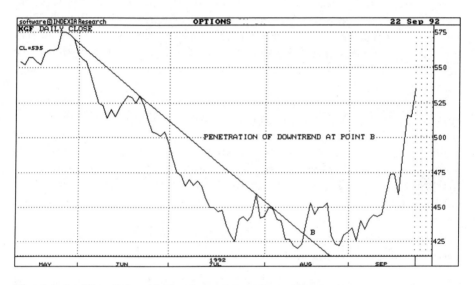

Chart 2.6   Kingfisher daily close, May–September 1992

The weekly long-term chart for Sainsbury (Chart 2.7) again shows the long-term trend intact with three points of contact. As at 23 September 1992 the uptrend was still intact and this was also confirmed by the longer-term filters I89, I116. These are Indexia's 89-day and 116-day filters. (see Chart 2.8). At this date, no defensive action was therefore necessary and, if one was a holder of the shares, the only action to take would be perhaps to enhance income by writing out of the money puts against the stock.

Finally in this section, Chart 2.9 for Barclays illustrates the uptrend formation from April 1992 to the end of May 1992. It was then broken at

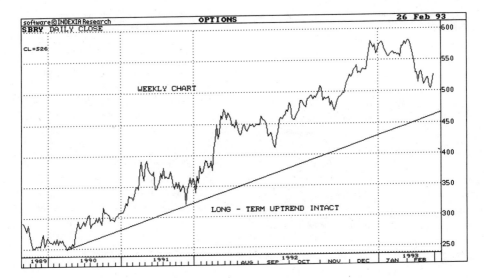

Chart 2.7   Sainsbury weekly chart, 1987–August 92

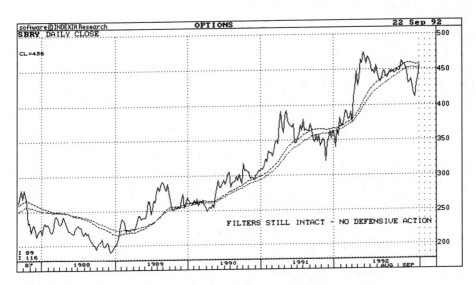

Chart 2.8   Sainsbury weekly close, 1987–September 1992

point S and a rapid decline followed. Chart 2.10 for Hanson illustrates two clearly defined uptrends and their eventual break downs, which again led to a rapid decline in the share price.

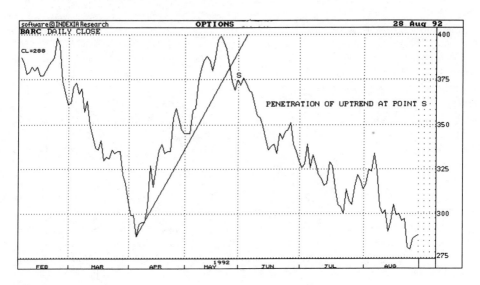

Chart 2.9   Barclays daily close, February–August 1992

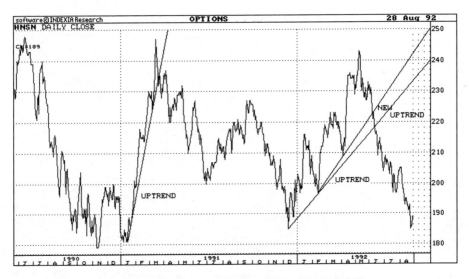

Chart 2.10   Hanson daily close, June 1990–August 1992

TREND CHANNELS

Trend channels occur when a line is drawn parallel to the main trend line
and the price bounces off and between these two parallel lines. The break
out can often be determined by the closer proximity of the price to the

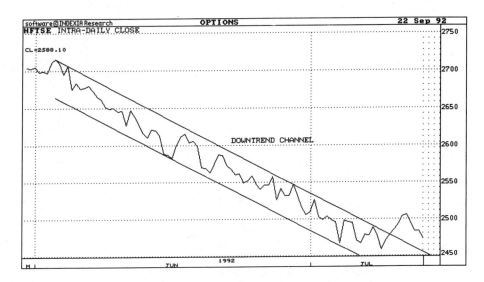

Chart 2.11 FTSE 100 intra-daily close, June–July 1992

upside of the parallels, when an upside break out usually occurs, or vice versa when the price begins to draw closer to the lower parallel and a downside break out generally occurs.

Chart 2.11 for the FTSE 100 (four-hourly input) illustrates a clear downtrend formation from June 1992 to the middle of July 1992. The upside break out can be anticipated as the price begins to move away from the lower parallel and closer to the upper parallel in the middle of July. However, it was important to realize that the major sell was still in place, since the FTALL daily chart had failed to give a major buy at this stage.

Similarly, Chart 2.12 shows a trend channel is in existence by drawing the basic downtrend from the highs and then drawing a lower parallel line to the main trend line. The lower parallel is drawn from the first prominent trough. Once the analyst has identified a trend channel then this can be used to advantage by going short once the price bounces off the upper trend line. However, I would be careful of going long when the price bounces off the lower parallel in a downtrend channel since, in effect, you are 'bucking the trend' which is not usually very wise! As with all trend lines, the longer it remains in contact and the more points of contact there are, then the more reliable it becomes. If a downtrend is in existence and this is broken on the downside, then it represents an acceleration of the downtrend.

Looking again at Chart 2.12 for BT, one can see that the move failed to reach the lower parallel line of the trend channel at the end of December and this usually indicates that the break out of the trend channel will be

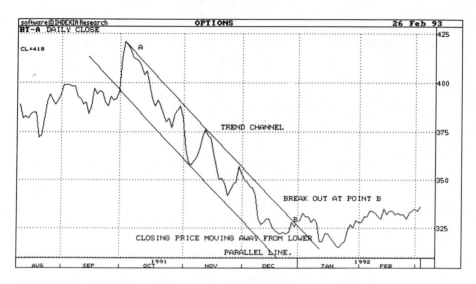

software ® INDEXIA Research   **OPTIONS**   26 Feb 93
BT-A DAILY CLOSE   425

CL=418   A

                                                                        400

                                    TREND CHANNEL   375

                                                                        350

                                    BREAK OUT AT POINT B

                                        B   325
        CLOSING PRICE MOVING AWAY FROM LOWER
                PARALLEL LINE.
   AUG   SEP   OCT   NOV   DEC   JAN   FEB
                        1991   1992

Chart 2.12   BT daily close, August 1991–February 1992

on the upside, which in this case it was. Some analysts also use the width of the trend channel to measure the distance of the anticipated break out.

The channel line, or the return line as it is often called, is another useful variation of the trend line technique. These patterns consist of two parallel lines, slanting upwards for an uptrend channel with the price oscillating between the two parallel lines while the upper parallel line acts as a resistance level.

Trend channels can be very useful tools for the chartist in the trade options market. For instance, when the share price bounces off its lower parallel line, this could be an opportunity to step in and buy some call options. Whereas if the share price reacts downwards from the upper parallel resistance line, then this would be an opportunity to close the call and take the profit. The same principle applies in reverse to a downtrend channel.

An example of an uptrend channel with a break out on the downside is shown in Chart 2.13. Note the price is moving away from the upper parallel but, eventually, a new upward movement was established when the resistance level at 95p was overcome.

Support and resistance

When I previously discussed the trend, I stated that prices move in a series of peaks and troughs and the direction of these peaks and troughs determine the trend of the market. The troughs are known as support and this is indicative of an area where a level of support is found which

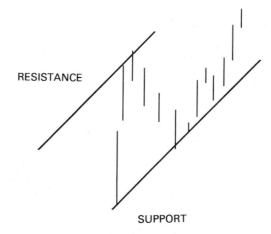

attracts more buyers into the market. As a result, the buyers gain the upper hand and this halts any further declines.

Resistance is the opposite of support and represents a price level or area over the market where selling pressure overcomes buying pressure and a price advance is turned back.

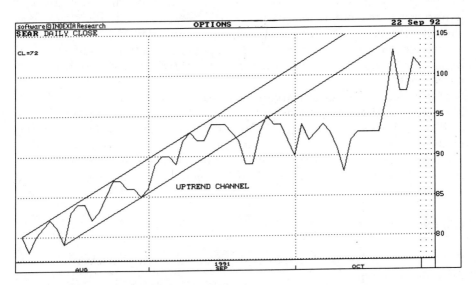

Chart 2.13 Sears daily close, August–October 1992

Another example of a downtrend in existence is illustrated by the bar chart of the FTSE 100 (Chart 2.14) when a parallel line is drawn to the main downtrend line. One can see that the FTSE moved within a fairly well-defined downtrend channel. A warning signal was given in the middle of August that this downtrend channel was about to be penetrated

Chart 2.14   FTSE 100 daily bar chart, May–September 1992

as prices began to move away from the lower parallel and make a temporary break out through the upper trend line. At this stage, you should have been put on your guard and begun reducing your exposure to any written calls or closing out any open put positions. The eventual break out came at the beginning of September with a rapid upward movement.

The purpose of this example is therefore two-fold. First, you should have been noticing that the downtrend was beginning to look very fragile as closing prices were pulling away from the lower parallel. Secondly, many traders have informed me that they received a major buy signal in the middle of August but were caught out when the market retreated a further 80 points. How could this have been avoided? Here is just one suggestion.

Bar chart construction

Bar Charts can be constructed to show daily, weekly or even monthly price fluctuations.

In order to construct a bar chart, you simply mark on your chart paper: a dot to mark the highest price at which the share/index was traded that day and another dot to mark the lowest price traded for the day. You then join up the dots with a vertical line to show the range of the day and mark a horizontal line across the vertical line showing the closing price.

Some analysts mark the closing price to the right of the vertical line and the opening price to the left of the vertical line.

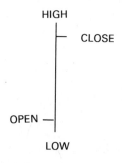

HIGH

├─ CLOSE

OPEN ─┤

LOW

BAR CHART

DIRECTIONAL MOVEMENT AND OVERBOUGHT/OVERSOLD INDICATORS

Using a directional movement indicator measured over 14 days (Wells Wilder Standard 14-Day), if you wait for the plus line (+DI) to cross above the minus line (−DI) then the uptrend is confirmed. The directional movement indicator ('DMI') was designed to capitalize on trending markets and will be discussed in more detail later on in the book.

Welles wilder directional movement indicator

The concept behind this indicator is to determine when a particular market is in a trending mode. In other words how much directional movement there is in the market. The DMI (ADX) line – Average Directional Index – is measured on a scale of 0–100. The higher the value of the ADX line, the stronger the trend whether up or down.

Two further lines are generated by the DMI:

1. DI +Ve
2. DI −ve.

The first line measures positive upwards movement and indicates what percentage of the true range over the period selected is up movement. The second number measures negative (downward movement) and indicates what percentage of the true range over the period selected is down movement.

A buy signal is given when the +DI crosses over the −DI line and a sell signal is given when it crosses below the −DI line.

The purpose at this stage of the book is to highlight the main trends and then start to combine other indicators to confirm break outs and the establishment of new trends. Chart 2.15 shows that the DMI confirmed the new uptrend for the FTSE when it made its crossover on 11 September

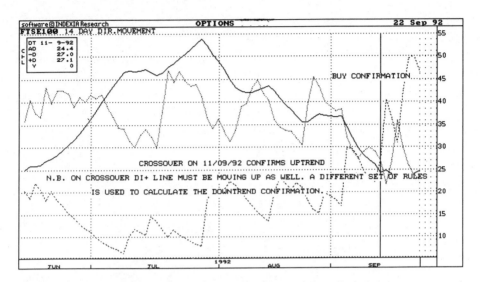

Chart 2.15 FTSE 100 14-day directional movement indicator, June–September 1992

1992 with the FTSE standing at 2370. It is important to point out that we could also use other indicators to assist us in determining the existence of a new trend: I find the INDEXIA filters and volume indicators particularly useful and these will be discussed more fully later in the book. My aim here is to introduce readers to the main concepts, with detailed analysis coming later.

The other secondary indicator I will mention briefly at this stage is the overbought/oversold ('OB/OS') indicator which can be used for optimizing entry into the market – particularly useful if you are trading the derivatives market. As Chart 2.16 for the FTSE clearly shows, although the position trade proved to be absolutely correct there was still a substantial pull back after the major buy and, if you are trading the futures market, you may find this somewhat hazardous and emotionally strenuous. Therefore it may be necessary and prudent to use the five-day OB/OS indicator for this type of trading (see Chart 2.17).

Overbought/oversold indicators

This indicator shows the percentage by which the price is above (or below) the moving average selected.

When the price reaches certain percentage levels away from the moving average, it is said either to be overbought (if positive) or oversold (if negative). When this happens, the chances are that the price will correct to rectify the situation. Basically, what the indicator is telling us is that a

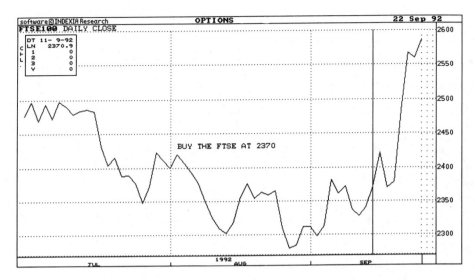

Chart 2.16 FTSE 100 daily close, July–September 1992

point is reached where this greatly accelerated momentum of buying (overbought) or selling (oversold) can no longer be maintained and has no option but to reverse.

The overbought/oversold index is again a trend and, as long as the line keeps on rising even when in an overbought zone, no trend reversal need occur. It is only when the moving total 'tops out' inside the overbought zone (or 'bottoms out' in the oversold zone) and begins to decline, that a secondary reaction, or at best, a period of consolidation can be expected within a short time.

Historically, with the OB/OS indicator showing a reading of two or more, then a correction in the market is likely. In this case, using the five-day OB/OS indicator, the entry into the market would have been delayed until 16 September at 2378, and with no pull back!

Chart 2.18 for RTZ clearly shows a strong support line at connecting points E, F, G and H. The uptrend channel is formed by drawing a parallel line to this support line. An eventual break out came at the end of April with a new steeper uptrend (1–2). The break out of this steeper uptrend came at point S which proved to be an accurate assessment.

Chart 2.19 provides examples of a steep uptrend and of downtrends. Notice the downtrends are now forming a reversed fan formation with an early warning sign that this downtrend may be coming to an end with the first penetration of the latest downtrend at the end of August.

Another example of a clear, strong downtrend is seen in Chart 2.20. There is break out at point C and then a fall back to point 1 with the original resistance line of the downtrend supporting the new uptrend.

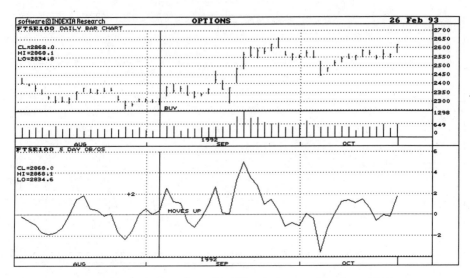

Chart 2.17   FTSE 100 five-day OB/OS, August–October 1992

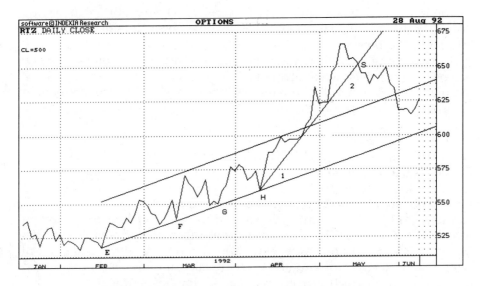

Chart 2.18   RTZ daily close, January–June 1992

Chart 2.21 provides another example of a clear downtrend A–B with eventual break out at point B on 9 April at 419p. The only caveat I would suggest here, is that unless the FTSE 100 Index has given a major buy then I would be hesitant of purchasing shares or taking up options on break out share formations by themselves. However, as stated earlier, if the

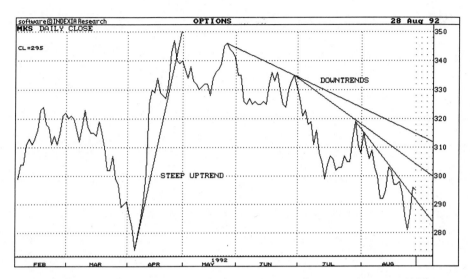

Chart 2.19 Marks and Spencer daily close, February–August 1992

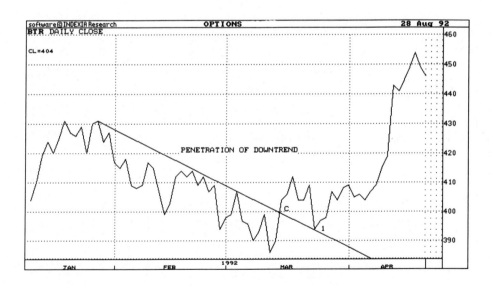

Chart 2.20 BTR daily close, January–April 1992

FTSE is already in a buy mode then this break out would be a confirmation signal. In this instance the break out proved to be correct, but principles of prudent trading should be adhered to.

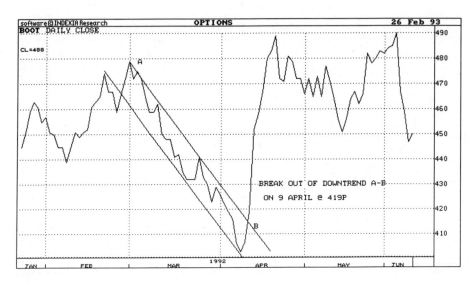

Chart 2.21   Boots daily close, January–June 1992

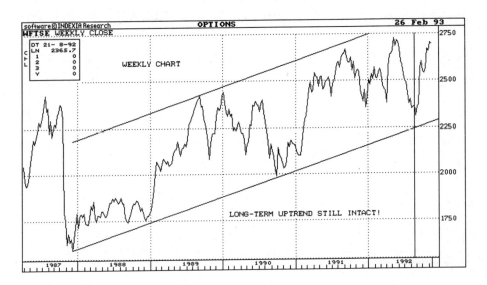

Chart 2.22   FTSE 100 weekly close, 1987–92

Chart 2.22 is a weekly chart for the FTSE and the long-term uptrend is still intact. Clear buying opportunities in the market are certainly appearing around the 2250–2300 level and this should prove to be a strong support level.

SPEED LINES

The ⅓ and ⅔ speed lines or, as they are sometimes called, speed resistance lines, are used for finding areas of support and resistance during uptrends and downtrends. They are termed 'speed lines' because they measure slope, which is, in effect, speed of a price movement in a given direction. The ⅓ and ⅔ speed lines indicate a slope which is one-third and two-thirds of the slope of the initial trend. During an uptrend, the price (or any indicator) can be expected to find support during a correction on first the ⅔ and secondly the ⅓ speed line drawn from the bottom. If the price does not hold at the ⅓ line then a major correction can be expected.

For example, a price breaking the ⅔ line but finding support at the ⅓ line will be resisted by the ⅔ line when it attempts to rally back again. A break of this resistance can be considered to be bullish. A price that breaches the ⅔ and then the ⅓ will often rally to the ⅓ before continuing its decline. (The above points apply conversely to downtrends as well.)

Chart 2.23   FTSE 100 intra-daily close, January–September 1992

Chart 2.23 for the FTSE 100 (fixed hour input) shows that the ⅔ speed line was broken in the middle of September, although it did fall back initially. But this provided a clear warning signal and eventual confirmation that the previous downtrend was in jeopardy and, indeed, was confirmed on the next upside penetration. Speed lines should not be used as buy or sell signals in the market, but rather as identification of support and resistance levels and warning signals that previous trends are in jeopardy.

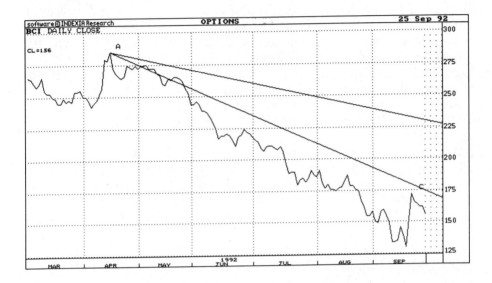

Chart 2.24   Blue Circle daily close, March–September 1992

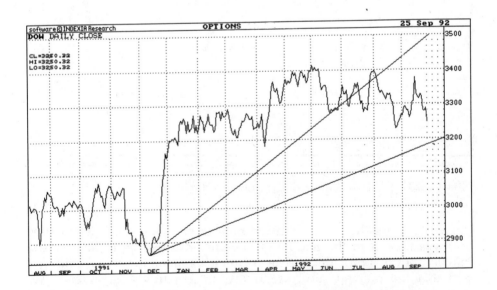

Chart 2.25   Dow Jones daily close, August 1991–September 1992

Chart 2.26   British Airways weekly close, 1987–92

Chart 2.24 for Blue Circle shows the speed line from the high at point A to the low point in the middle of September 1992. The ⅔ speed line at end-September is showing resistance with the closing price moving away at point C.

Chart 2.25 shows that the closing price for the Dow Jones was moving through the ⅔ speed line at the beginning of July, and was eventually confirmed at the beginning of August, with possible support coming in at 3200. If the price moves down through the 3200 level then a major correction downwards could be imminent.

The weekly chart for British Airways (Chart 2.26) shows the speed line drawn from the low at point A to the high at 315p. The ⅔ speed line was broken at point B and then retraced to point C, where resistance came into play.

FAN FORMATIONS

Another interesting feature which develops from trend lines is the 'fan formation'. Fan formations are so called simply because when they open they look like a fan.

In order to draw a fan formation you take (for an uptrend) a major low point and connect the trend line with the first major correction. You then take the same low point and connect the next trend line with the next secondary low, and so on, until you have four trend lines drawn one below the other.

The concept is that once the closing price falls through the primary trend line then this is a warning signal that the uptrend is in jeopardy. On the downside, breaking through the secondary trend line means that long positions should be closed out or, at the very least, protected by writing calls against the stock or purchasing put options on the market index: by the time the price has fallen through the the third trend line it is usually too late and a major new downtrend is in existence. Sometimes, however, you do get a second chance to bail out on the penetration of the third trend line in the fan formation, and then the fourth trend line really is your last chance!

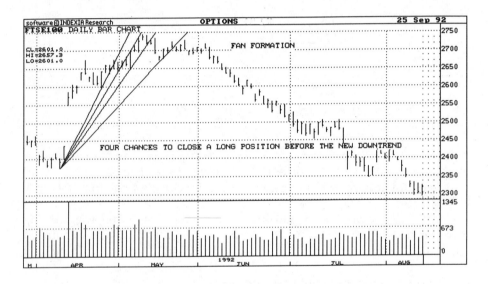

Chart 2.27   FTSE 100 daily bar chart, April–August 1992

The daily bar chart for the FTSE 100 (Chart 2.27) clearly shows the uptrend formation from the beginning of April and a fan formation developing from the beginning of May, based on the low point at the beginning of April. The last chance to close any long positions was heralded at the end of May when the FTSE's closing price went down through the fourth uptrend line. This, together with the other technical indicators I use, such as 'on balance volume' and INDEXIA filters, confirmed to me that this latest uptrend was finished and a new downtrend was emerging. The study of volume is very important and, as most experienced analysts know, 'volume leads price'. (Volume will be discussed in more detail in Chapters 5 and 8.)

On balance volume

On Balance Volume was developed and popularized by Joseph Granville in 1963. OBV produces a volume line curve which can be used to either confirm the current trend or to anticipate a reversal of the current trend by diverging from the price curve itself.

Construction

Total volume for each day is assigned a plus or minus value depending on whether prices are closing higher or lower for that day. A higher close causes the volume indicators to be assigned a plus value while a lower close would give the volume indicator a negative value.

A running cumulative total is then deduced by adding or subtracting each day's volume based on the direction of the market close. It is the direction of the OBV indicator that is important. If the trend for the market is up, then the OBV should also be making higher tops and bottoms (ie trading up). It is when the OBV fails to confirm this uptrend and moves downwards to form a pattern of lower tops and bottoms, while the market continues to move up, that divergence occurs. This is an impending warning that the uptrend for the market could be coming to an end.

Similarily, in reverse, once the downtrend had been established then a reverse fan formation can be seen for the FTSE (Chart 2.28), with an initial

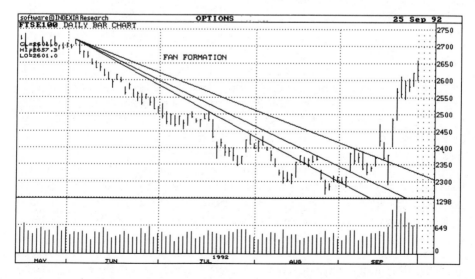

Chart 2.28 FTSE 100 daily bar chart, May–September 1992

breakthrough on the upside of the first downtrend line in the middle of August. This action should have sounded warning bells and, when the second downtrend line was finally breached at the beginning of September, then all short positions should have been closed. This second downside trend line at first proved to be a resistance level to the new uptrend, but eventually the buyers got the upper hand and a new uptrend emerged.

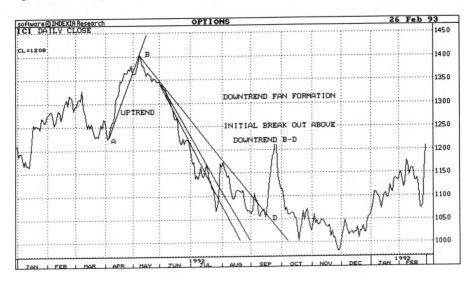

Chart 2.29   ICI daily close, January 1992–February 1993

Chart 2.29 for ICI highlights the uptrend AB but, more importantly, the downtrend from the high point B with a reverse fan formation unfolding. A possible buy could have been activated at the end of July, because the secondary downtrend line had been breached, but, as mentioned earlier, I prefer to purchase stock only when the major buy has been confirmed by the FTSE 100 as well, and this did not happen until 11 September 1992. As at 27 August the third downtrend line had not been penetrated and neither had the FTSE 100 given a major buy signal.

However, if we now move ICI's chart on to include the closing prices for September (see Chart 2.30), we can clearly see that the share price moved above the third downtrend line and I can confirm that the FTSE was also in a major buy mode. A prudent trade would have been to buy ICI shares or call options on the shares on 11 September 1992.

Again I must stress these are not the only indicators that I would use to confirm the major buy signal for the FTSE or a share but, for current purposes, the indicators that have been discussed so far do constitute a

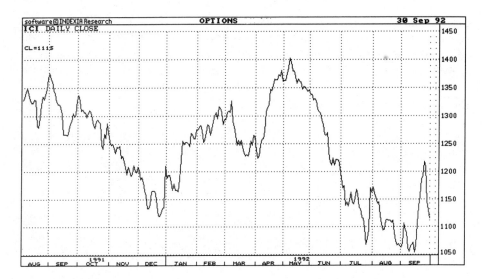

Chart 2.30   ICI daily close, August–September 1992

major part of that signal. Secondary indicators can and do play an important part also, especially for optimizing the timing of entry and exit from the market, and they will be discussed in Chapter 4.

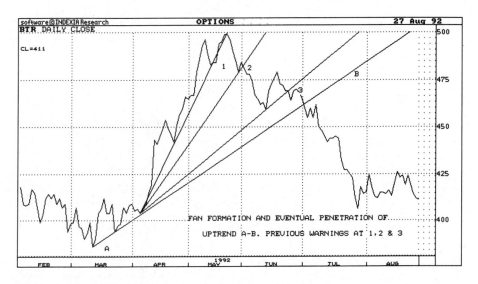

Chart 2.31   BTR daily close, February–August 1992

Chart 2.31 shows a typical fan formation for BTR – eventual penetration of the fan towards the end of May, followed by one last chance at the end of June at point 3. The penetration of the uptrend line (1) was a warning signal and one should have sold the shares or at least protected them with written calls at the end of May. Chart 2.32 provides a further example of fan formation and a downtrend channel.

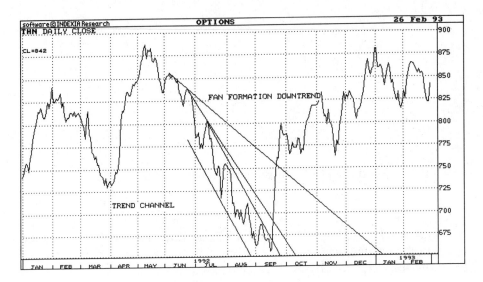

Chart 2.32   THN daily close, January 1992–February 1993

Finally, Chart 2.33 shows an example of an uptrend fan formation with three opportunities to sell or protect the share price for Shell. Ideally, one should have at least taken some action in the early part of June.

Fibonacci

Leonardo Fibonacci was a thirteen-century Italian mathematician, who discovered a number sequence to which he gave his name, the Fibonacci numbers. In his book *Liber Abaci* (Book of Calculations), he presents the Fibonacci sequence as a solution to a mathematical problem involving the reproduction rate of rabbits. The number sequence is 1,1,2,3,5,8,13,21,34,55,89,144 etc. The main points of consideration are:

1. The sum of any two consecutive numbers equals the next higher number (eg $5 + 8 = 13$).
2. The ratio of any number to the higher number next to it approaches 0.618 after the first four numbers (eg $1/1 = 1.00$, $1/2 = 0.50$; $2/3 = 0.67$, $3/5 = 0.60$; $5/8 = 0.625$, $8/13 = 0.615$; $13/21 = 0.619$ etc).

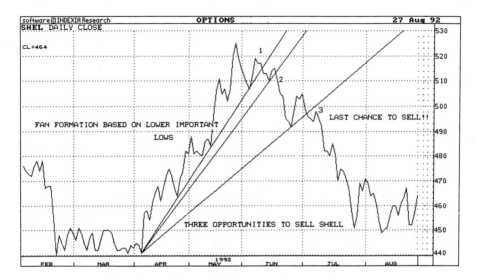

Chart 2.33   Shell daily close, February–August 1992

3. The ratio of any number to the lower number next to it is approximately 1.1618.
4. The ratio of alternate numbers approaches 2.618 or its inverse 0.382.

The Fibonacci relationships seem to recur throughout nature, existing in many areas of human activity.

Fibonacci fan lines

The Fibonacci number series is the basis for the system called Fibonacci fan lines. The ratios of 0.618 and 0.382 are important to Elliot Wave theorists, who look for the price to correct from the original trend by these amounts. The 0.5 ratio (the ratio of the second two Fibonacci numbers, 1 and 2) is also important.

The Fibonacci fan lines are constructed automatically by defining a high and a low point or a low and a high point in the price action. The slope of the trend between these two points is calculated and the three Fibonacci lines are drawn, reflecting the slopes which are 0.618, 0.5 and 0.382 of the original trend. The fan lines are therefore not simple retracements from the defined high or low but are retracements from an *imaginary* high or low which would have been achieved had the original trend remained in place.

Fibonacci fan lines are different from the straight retracement fan formations previously described, which are constant retracements measured from the high or low. This often equates to the second trend line in the ordinary fan formation.

Elliot wave principle

There are three aspects of wave theory. In order of importance, these are:

1. pattern
2. ratio
3. time

I will not attempt to explain the Elliot Wave principle in full, but suffice to say there are many books devoted to this subject alone. The *pattern*, however, refers to the wave pattern of formations that comprise the most important element of the theory. *Ratio* analysis is useful in determining retracement points and price objectives by measuring the relationship between the different waves.

Finally, *time* relationships also exist and can be used to confirm the wave patterns and ratios.

The basic premise is that the market follows a principle of five wave advances followed by a three wave decline. Each cycle consists of eight waves.

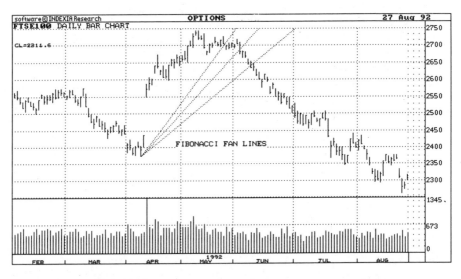

Chart 2.34   FTSE 100 daily bar chart, February–August 1992

Chart 2.34 for the FTSE 100 shows the Fibonacci fan lines drawn from the low point in the middle of April 1992 to the high point at just below 2750 at the beginning of May. The signal to at least close long positions was given towards the end of May when the FTSE Index moved down through the first Fibonacci fan line. You should certainly not be long of the market once the second Fibonacci fan line is penetrated (at the beginning of June 1992) and, by the use of other indicators, you should have already opened put positions on the Index and/or protected stocks by writing calls against them.

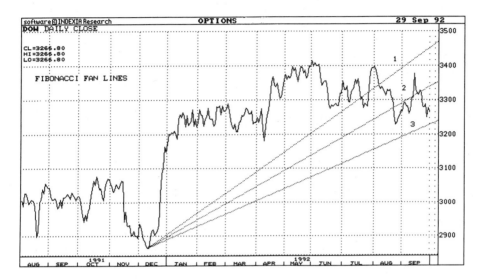

Chart 2.35 Dow Jones daily close, August 1991–September 1992

Chart 2.35 highlights the closing price for the Dow Jones Index from August 1991 to September 1992, with the Fibonacci fan lines overdrawn from the low point in December 1991 to the high point at the end of May 1992. The lines confirm that long positions in the Dow should have been liquidated at the end of July 1992.

The volume indicators can also assist in determining when long positions should be liquidated. Don't forget that volume leads price and if the price is rising but volume is falling then this information, coupled with the Fibonacci fan lines, starts to build up an overall picture that enables you to make some important and correct decisions about the market.

Chart 2.36 shows the Fibonacci fan formation drawn from the low at the beginning of April to the high at the end of May. On penetration of the first fan line, then all long positions should have been liquidated (see Chart 2.36 at the middle of June). Similarly, in reverse, once the share price has been moving down for some time (see Chart 2.37) then on penetration of the first Fibonacci fan line drawn from a high to a low point, all short positions should have been liquidated at the beginning of September and, by the use of other chosen indicators such as volume, INDEXIA filters and secondary oscillators, an optimum entry for the purchase of shares in Shell at around 465p–470p should have been

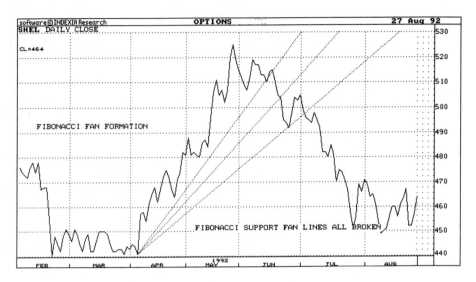

Chart 2.36   Shell daily close, February–August 1992

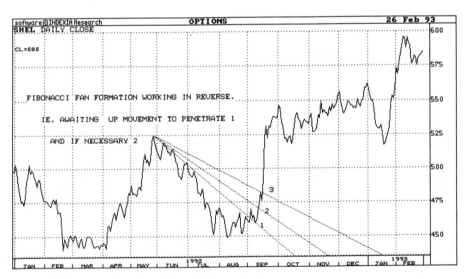

Chart 2.37   Shell daily close, January 1992–February 1993 – reverse fan formation

highlighted. Chart 2.38 illustrates the actual movement of the Shell share price from the beginning of September once the price had moved up through the first Fibonacci fan line.

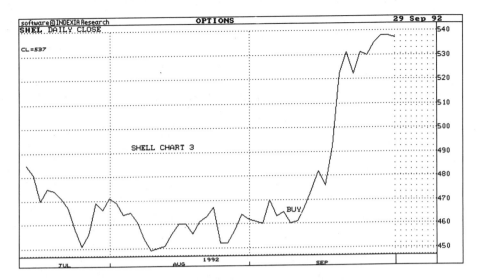

Chart 2.38 Shell daily close, July–September 1992

You will have noticed that we have often touched on the subject of the INDEXIA filters over the last two chapters, and how these can assist in timing of exit and entry into the market. Chapter 3 will now discuss these unique filters in more detail, together with the moving average convergence divergence indicator.

3

Filters, Moving Averages and the MACD Indicator

Moving averages are perhaps the oldest technical tool available to traders. But although this indicator works well in a trending market, when the market is in a fairly tight trading range then the results can be disastrous with a number of whiplash movements occurring. This can be illustrated with an example of the FTSE 100, using a 10 and 20-day moving average. During the period from April 1992 to September 1992 (see Chart 3.1) the Index was trending very well and consequently the 10 and 20-day moving averages worked reasonably well.

However, if you look at Chart 3.2 for the FTSE 100 during the period from March to July 1991, the market was trading in a fairly tight trading range and the moving averages did not work so well. In fact, whiplash

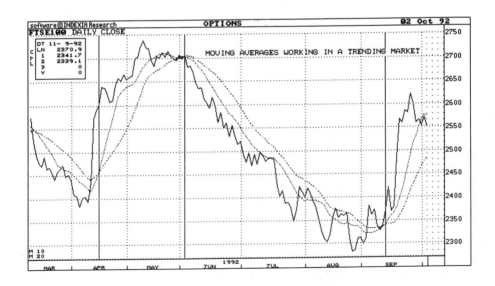

Chart 3.1   FTSE 100 daily close, March–September 1992

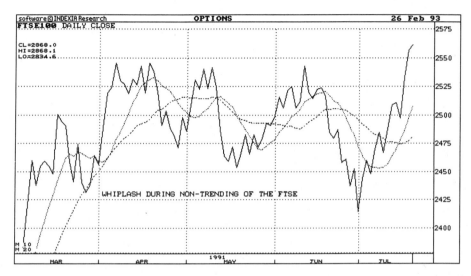

Chart 3.2 FTSE 100 daily close, March–July 1991

movements occurred on a number of occasions, and it was not until the
market started to trend again at the beginning of July that the moving
averages began to work again.

To try and overcome the whiplash effect, many analysts now use the
exponential moving average which assigns a greater weight to recent
figures (see Chart 3.3). For instance if a six-day weighted average is
chosen, the sixth price is multiplied by six, the fifth price by five, the
fourth price by four, etc. All the resultant values are then added together
and divided. The longer the period, the greater the weighting factor.

The choice and type of moving average is a personal decision and
depends on the time cycle you wish to trade. In the traded options
market, many analysts prefer to use shorter-term averages which in turn
favour shorter-term trading patterns. Moving averages when used in
conjuction with other indicators are one of the most powerful tools
available to the technical analyst, but which moving average to use, what
type and how many, are practically impossible questions to answer unless
you have access to an optimization program. I personally have found such
programs invaluable and, historically, a trade summary can also be
produced for any file so you can see exactly where and when the signals
were given, as well as the profits on each trade. (For further information
on this optimisation programme, please refer to the INDEXIA Moving
Average Manager Program in Chapter 6).

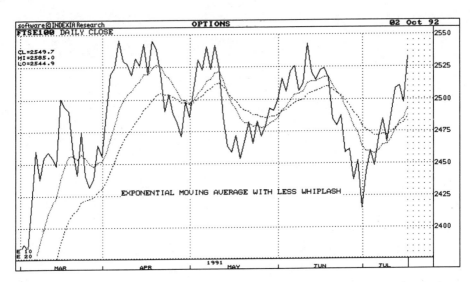

Chart 3.3   FTSE 100 daily close, March–July 1991 (exponential moving average)

USING MOVING AVERAGES AND FILTERS

As mentioned earlier in this book, in my opinion a single indicator should not be used by itself to generate buy and sell signals, but rather a combination of indicators to build up a picture that gives you confidence to trade your system. Let's now look at some examples of moving averages in practice.

Chart 3.4 illustrates the daily close for Bass with the 10 and 25-day moving averages overlaid. I have also illustrated the corresponding printout which details the buy and sell signals for these moving averages, together with the profits from 17 June 1986 to 17 September 1992. Using two simple moving averages over this period, which have been optimized, produced an overall profit of 42 per cent on the long side and 11 per cent on the short side. However, Chart 3.5 highlights the buy and sell signals using the optimized INDEXIA filters.

Not only are there fewer trades carried out but the overall profitability has increased dramatically as well, to 93 per cent on the long side and 60 per cent on the short side.

A further improvement can also be considered. I personally will only go long of a stock when the FTSE itself has given a major buy signal and, similarly, will only go short when the major sell for the FTSE is in place also. For instance, when the major buy for the FTSE was given on 31 January 1991, (utilizing my trading rules) I would have ignored the signals given by the filters to go long of Bass on 21 November 1990 and also on 6

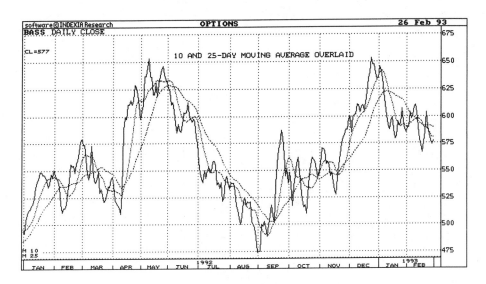

```
UK OPTIONS                            HISTORIC TRADE SUMMARY              06 Oct 92
<---------------LONG----------------->  <----------------SHORT------------
<----open---->  <----close---->    %    <----open---->  <----close---->

BASS       SIMPLE   10  25  0 1606 0         SIMPLE   10  25  0 1606 0

170686     390  240686    394   1.0   240686     394  250686    403  -2
250686     403  140786    382  -5.2   140786     382  030986    388  -1
030986     388  190986    365  -5.9   190986     365  241086    348   4
241086     348  281186    369   6.0   281186     369  301286    370  -0
301286     370  010487    443  19.7   010487     443  300487    470  -5
300487     470  020787    493   4.9   020787     493  090787    519  -5
090787     519  290787    503  -3.1   290787     503  040987    477   5
040987     477  091087    480   0.6   091087     480  041287    391  22
041287     391  111287    391   0.0   111287     391  161287    404  -3
161287     404  140188    396  -2.0   140188     396  250288    405  -2
250288     405  060488    414   2.2   060488     414  020588    423  -2
020588     423  110588    411  -2.8   110588     411  170688    403   2
170688     403  280688    394  -2.2   280688     394  080888    394   0
080888     394  120888    388  -1.5   120888     388  270988    388   0
270988     388  231188    400   3.1   231188     400  281288    399   0
281288     399  200389    463  16.0   200389     463  260489    470  -1
260489     470  060689    469  -0.2   060689     469  150689    497  -5
150689     497  070989    557  12.1   070989     557  110989    555   0
110989     555  190989    531  -4.3   190989     531  131189    496   7
131189     496  250190    512   3.2   250190     512  020490    469   9
020490     469  240490    449  -4.3   240490     449  100590    487  -5
100590     487  160790    555  14.0   160790     555  180790    554   0
180790     554  070890    531  -4.2   070890     531  101090    516   2
101090     516  071190    504  -2.3   071190     504  271190    516  -2
271190     516  100191    524   1.6   100191     524  200291    493   0
200291     493  250391    499   1.2   250391     499  260491    478   4
260491     478  170591    475  -0.6   170591     475  310591    496  -4
310591     496  210691    472  -4.8   210691     472  220791    462   2
220791     462  010891    462   0.0   010891     462  220891    467  -1
220891     467  240991    488   4.5   240991     488  011091    515  -5
011091     515  211091    496  -3.7   211091     496  151191    484   2
151191     484  191191    473  -2.3   191191     473  131291    500  -5
131291     500  110292    515   3.0   110292     515  250292    560  -8
250292     560  170392    549  -2.0   170392     549  130492    599  -8
130492     599  050692    605   1.0   050692     605  170992    537  12
170992     537  061092    536  -0.2
                        Total 42.5                        Total  11
------------------------------------------------------------------------
copyright (C) INDEXIA Research
```

Chart 3.4 BASS daily close, January 1992–February 1993 (and simple average trade summary)

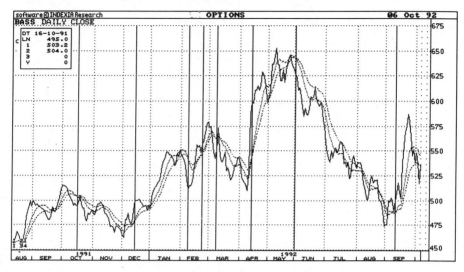

UK OPTIONS				HISTORIC TRADE SUMMARY					06 Oct 92

<---------------LONG----------------->   <---------------SHORT------------>
<----open-----> <----close---->   %   <----open-----> <----close---->

BASS	INDEXIA	14	28	0 1606 0	INDEXIA	14	28	0 1606 0
050686	390	110686	383	-1.8	110686	383	170686	390	-1
170686	390	070786	388	-0.5	070786	388	180886	379	2
180886	379	280886	368	-2.9	280886	368	010986	375	-1
010986	375	170986	365	-2.7	170986	365	161086	350	4
161086	350	011286	364	4.0	011286	364	301286	370	-1
301286	370	200387	465	25.7	200387	465	280487	469	-0
280487	469	040687	494	5.3	040687	494	150687	513	-3
150687	513	230687	494	-3.7	230687	494	100787	525	-5
100787	525	200787	510	-2.9	200787	510	010987	463	10
010987	463	071087	485	4.8	071087	485	231187	390	24
231187	390	130188	395	1.3	130188	395	170288	396	-0
170288	396	300388	423	6.8	300388	423	130688	404	4
130688	404	280688	394	-2.5	280688	394	120788	395	-0
120788	395	190788	389	-1.5	190788	389	280788	394	-1
280788	394	120888	388	-1.5	120888	388	180888	394	-1
180888	394	250888	381	-3.3	250888	381	190988	375	1
190988	375	141188	399	6.4	141188	399	201288	399	0
201288	399	180289	465	16.5	180289	465	200289	473	-1
200289	473	030389	483	2.1	030389	483	250489	464	4
250489	464	310589	472	1.7	310589	472	150689	497	-5
150689	497	240789	515	3.6	240789	515	020889	539	-4
020889	539	140889	538	-0.2	140889	538	170889	553	-2
170889	553	290889	540	-2.4	290889	540	071189	478	13
071189	478	050190	522	9.2	050190	522	230390	474	10
230390	474	240490	449	-5.3	240490	449	300490	468	-4
300490	468	210690	547	16.9	210690	547	051090	487	12
051090	487	051190	508	4.3	051190	508	211190	517	-1
211190	517	041290	498	-3.7	041290	498	061290	518	-3
061290	518	030191	517	-0.2	030191	517	140291	482	7
140291	482	210391	510	5.8	210391	510	230491	480	6
230491	480	190691	480	0.0	190691	480	160791	468	2
160791	468	170991	480	2.6	170991	480	270991	503	-4
270991	503	111091	495	-1.6	111091	495	061291	487	1
061291	487	050292	540	10.9	050292	540	210292	548	-1
210292	548	060392	542	-1.1	060392	542	100492	588	-7
100492	588	190592	619	5.3	190592	619	030892	539	14
030892	539	100892	513	-4.8	100892	513	180892	518	-1
180892	518	260892	497	-4.1	260892	497	070992	503	-1
070992	503	061092	536	6.6					
		Total		93.2			Total		60

Chart 3.5   BASS daily close, August 1991–September 1992 (and INDEXIA trade summary)

December 1990, thus avoiding these losses. Since my overall strategy for the market (the FTSE) was still not telling me to go long of the market, these long positions would have been ignored and not traded. However, on 14 February 1991 when the filters again gave a buy signal for Bass, the FTSE buy signal was also in place and, in this instance, I would have gone long of Bass and this trade in turn would have proved to have been a profitable one.

Similarly with short positions. The signal for my overall short position for the market in 1992 was given on 1 June, and when the filters generated short signals for Bass on 6 March 1992 I would have ignored these. Admittedly, the next signal on 19 May proved to be correct at a share price of 619p, but again I would have waited until 1 June and the share price for Bass on this date was 626p – in fact a better price! By trading in this selective manner you not only cut the number of trades carried out, thus reducing the risk of overtrading but, more importantly, by sticking with the overall trend of the market you cut out those trades which in most cases are bucking the trend of the market and consequently result in losses.

A further example is provided by Ladbrokes (see Chart 3.6). Once again the filters produce better results than the simple moving averages. As the printout clearly illustrates, using a simple 39 and 42-day moving average the results and number of trades carried out between 1 August 1986 and 16 June 1992 show a profit of 38 per cent on the long side and 48 per cent on the short side. However, in this example I am also highlighting the fact that it is equally important to select the correct periods for the type of trading that you wish to carry out.

The next example (Chart 3.7) illustrates the daily close with the short 7 and 25-day filters overlaid. In this instance, although the overall profitability was high it did result in a vast number of trading positions being executed with some intervening losses as well. Personally, this type of trading does not suit me and I prefer to use the longer dated filters.

The longer-term 18 and 35-day filters once optimized (see Chart 3.8) give a 92 per cent profit on the long side and a 117 per cent profit on the short side.

Again as previously discussed, I would not buck the overall trend of the market and would only obey those signals which are in line with the overall buy or sell signals of the FTSE Index. For instance, the long signal given for Ladbrokes on 12 November 1991 which resulted in a 6.7 per cent loss would not have been traded, since the overall trend for the market was still down and the buy signal for the FTSE had yet to be activated.

Charts 3.9 and 3.10, plus the related printouts further demonstrate the effectiveness of these filters. But again I must stress that these are not the only signals that I would adhere to. Before actually trading, I would be looking at the indicators and trends discussed in Chapters 1 and 2 and

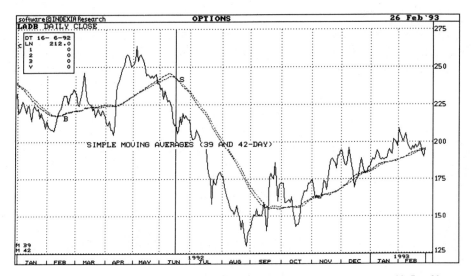

SPOT CURRENCY TRADING   HISTORIC TRADE SUMMARY   03 Jun 93

	<----open----->	<----close---->	%		<----open----->	<----close---->	
LADB	SIMPLE 39 42	0 1605 0			SIMPLE 39 42	0 1605 0		
010886	172	040886 170	-1.2		040886 170	270886	178	-4
270886	178	050986 183	2.8		050986 183	150986	176	
150986	176	081086 176	0.0		081086 176	091086	173	
091086	173	221086 175	1.2		221086 175	071186	189	-,
071186	189	141186 187	-1.1		141186 187	171186	185	1
171186	185	060187 192	3.8		060187 192	150187	200	-4
150187	200	100487 208	4.0		100487 208	110687	208	0
110687	208	240687 215	3.4		240687 215	010787	212	1
010787	212	030987 220	3.8		030987 220	220987	231	-4
220987	231	280987 230	-0.4		280987 230	011087	228	0
011087	228	221087 188	-17.5		221087 188	261087	163	15
261087	163	271087 165	1.2		271087 165	231287	171	-3
231287	171	241287 172	0.6		241287 172	311287	161	6
311287	161	110588 195	21.1		110588 195	200588	204	-4
200588	204	060688 218	6.9		060688 218	100688	217	0
100688	217	010888 219	0.9		010888 219	110888	224	-2
110888	224	290988 226	0.9		290988 226	251088	226	0
251088	226	301188 217	-4.0		301188 217	270189	246	-11
270189	246	030589 286	16.3		030589 286	080589	291	-1
080589	291	110589 287	-1.4		110589 287	170589	290	-1
170589	290	200789 314	8.3		200789 314	270789	315	-0
270789	315	021089 329	4.4		021089 329	051089	325	1
051089	325	191089 295	-9.2		191089 295	121289	315	-6
121289	315	160290 302	-4.1		160290 302	230490	275	9
230490	275	240490 275	0.0		240490 275	040590	275	0
040590	275	080590 280	1.8		080590 280	090590	277	1
090590	277	150590 295	6.5		150590 295	060690	317	-6
060690	317	080890 291	-8.2		080890 291	121190	269	8
121190	269	031290 264	-1.9		031290 264	111290	262	0
111290	262	121290 254	-3.1		121290 254	070391	263	-3
070391	263	100591 288	9.5		100591 288	190891	259	11
190891	259	230991 258	-0.4		230991 258	260991	260	-0
260991	260	041091 259	-0.4		041091 259	081091	257	0
081091	257	091091 255	-0.8		091091 255	151091	251	1
151091	251	171091 253	0.8		171091 253	070292	207	22
070292	207	120292 219	5.8		120292 219	140292	222	-1
140292	222	240292 229	3.2		240292 229	280292	233	-1
280292	233	020392 232	-0.4		020392 232	100392	246	-5
100392	246	130492 239	-2.8		130492 239	300492	251	-4
300492	251	060592 264	5.2		060592 264	120592	256	3
120592	256	160692 212	-17.2		160692 212	061092	159	33
		Total	38.2			Total	48	

Chart 3.6 Ladbrokes daily close, January 1992–February 1993 (and simple average trade summary)

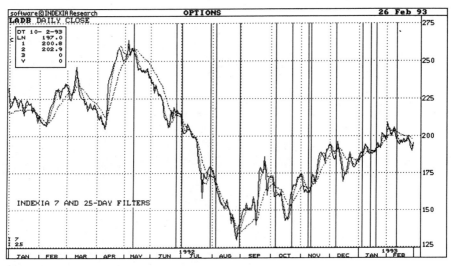

OPTIONS 26 Feb 93

LADB DAILY CLOSE

DT 10- 2-93
C LN 197.0
1 200.8
2 202.9
3 0
Y 0

INDEXIA 7 AND 25-DAY FILTERS

I 7
I 25

JAN | FEB | MAR | APR | MAY | JUN | 1992 JUL | AUG | SEP | OCT | NOV | DEC | JAN | 1993 FEB

	SPOT CURRENCY TRADIN								
	LONG				SHORT				
	open	close		%	open	close			
LADB	INDEXIA	7	25	0 1605 0		INDEXIA	7	25	0 1605 0
100786	183	180786	173	-5.5	130686	173	100786	183	-5
110886	177	110986	178	0.6	180786	173	110886	177	-2
171086	178	191186	182	2.2	110986	178	171086	178	0
151286	183	200187	197	7.7	191186	182	151286	183	-0
030287	203	230287	217	6.9	200187	197	030287	203	-3
020387	225	040387	221	-1.8	230287	217	020387	225	-3
230387	225	250387	221	-1.8	040387	221	230387	225	-1
270487	211	060587	196	-7.1	250387	221	270487	211	4
190587	211	110687	208	-1.4	060587	196	190587	211	-7
120687	218	230687	211	-3.2	110687	208	120687	218	-4
060787	216	220787	221	2.3	230687	211	060787	216	-2
240887	225	020987	218	-3.1	220787	221	240887	225	-1
070987	227	300987	227	0.0	020987	218	070987	227	-4
131087	243	191087	206	-15.2	300987	227	131087	243	-6
131187	158	311287	161	1.9	191087	206	131187	158	30
040188	169	270188	178	5.3	311287	161	040188	169	-4
280188	181	040288	177	-2.2	270188	178	280188	181	-1
170288	182	250388	200	9.9	040288	177	170288	182	-2
120488	207	150488	204	-1.4	250388	200	120488	207	-3
240588	204	200688	211	3.4	150488	204	240588	204	0
010888	219	230888	224	2.3	200688	211	010888	219	-3
270988	220	191088	227	3.2	230888	224	270988	220	1
211188	224	281188	220	-1.8	191088	227	211188	224	1
161288	217	220289	268	23.5	281188	220	161288	217	1
060389	279	080389	272	-2.5	220289	268	060389	279	-3
150389	280	160389	279	-0.4	080389	272	150389	280	-2
210489	274	310589	293	6.9	160389	279	210489	274	1
100789	299	100889	319	6.7	310589	293	100789	299	-2
040989	340	120989	337	-0.9	100889	319	040989	340	-6
031189	284	281189	291	2.5	120989	337	031189	284	18
301189	297	110190	335	12.8	281189	291	301189	297	-2
020390	298	060390	279	-6.4	110190	335	020390	298	12
150390	292	050490	289	-1.0	060390	279	150390	292	-4
080590	280	290690	339	21.1	050490	289	080590	280	3
300890	277	180990	261	-5.8	290690	339	300890	277	22
021090	246	311090	271	10.2	180990	261	021090	246	6
161190	274	031290	264	-3.6	311090	271	161190	274	-1
300191	226	220391	287	27.0	031290	264	300191	226	16
070591	284	140591	274	-3.5	220391	287	070591	284	1
110691	269	240691	255	-5.2	140591	274	110691	269	1
110791	250	190891	259	3.6	240691	255	110791	250	2
290891	279	100991	280	0.4	190891	259	290891	279	-7
181091	259	041191	248	-4.2	100991	280	181091	259	8
081191	255	261191	256	0.4	041191	248	081191	255	-2
271291	225	290192	214	-4.9	261191	256	271291	225	13
110292	215	040392	224	4.2	290192	214	110292	215	-0
060392	232	130392	226	-2.6	040392	224	060392	232	-3
100492	234	120592	256	9.4	130392	226	100492	234	-3
250692	218	010792	206	-5.5	120592	256	250692	218	17
300792	180	060892	162	-10.0	010792	206	300792	180	14
280892	141	061092	159	12.8	060892	162	280892	141	1
			Total	85.9				Total	9

Chart 3.7 Ladbrokes daily close, January 1992–February 1993 (and INDEXIA 7 and 25 trade summary)

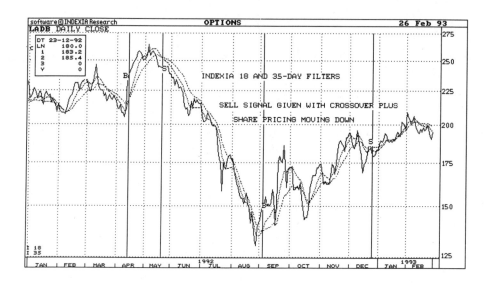

```
UK OPTIONS                          HISTORIC TRADE SUMMARY              06 Oct 92
<----------------LONG---------------->  <---------------SHORT--------------
<----open----->  <----close---->   %    <----open----->  <----close---->

LADB     INDEXIA  18   35   0 1605 0     INDEXIA  18   35   0 1605 0

100786     183    210786    170   -7.1   270686     173    100786    183    -5
120886     178    170986    177   -0.6   210786     170    120886    178    -4
291086     180    251186    180    0.0   170986     177    291086    180    -1
191286     186    060387    215   15.6   251186     180    191286    186    -3
280587     213    290687    212   -0.5   060387     215    280587    213     0
070787     222    060887    217   -2.3   290687     212    070787    222    -4
080987     227    191087    206   -9.3   060887     217    080987    227    -4
011287     146    100288    170   16.4   191087     206    011287     146   41
170288     182    010488    198    8.8   100288     170    170288    182    -6
030688     213    270688    213    0.0   010488     198    030688    213    -7
280688     217    300688    215   -0.9   270688     213    280688    217    -1
040888     221    300888    218   -1.4   300688     215    040888    221    -2
031088     224    011188    228    1.8   300888     218    031088    224    -2
301288     217    170389    273   25.8   011188     228    301288    217     5
030589     286    080689    293    2.4   170389     273    030589    286    -4
120789     312    210889    328    5.1   080689     293    120789    312    -6
050989     340    140989    338   -0.6   210889     328    050989    340    -3
101189     308    180190    324    5.2   140989     338    101189    308     9
220390     295    230490    275   -6.8   180190     324    220390     295    9
100590     288    050790    320   11.1   230490     275    100590    288    -4
051090     269    051290    260   -3.3   050790     320    051090    269    19
040291     230    110491    290   26.1   051290     260    040291    230    13
190791     244    180991    269   10.2   110491     290    190791    244    18
121191     262    281191    245   -6.5   180991     269    121191    262     2
060192     223    060292    208   -6.7   281191     245    060192    223     9
100292     211    200392    217    2.8   060292     208    100292     211   -1
130492     239    200592    243    1.7   200392     217    130492    239    -9
030992     151    061092    159    5.3   200592     243    030992    151    60
                       Total   92.6                            Total   117
```

Chart 3.8 Ladbrokes daily close, January 1992–February 1993 (and INDEXIA 18 and 35 trade summary)

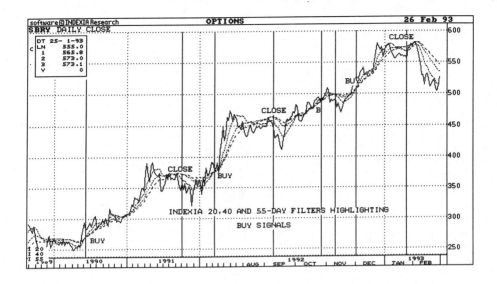

UK OPTIONS					HISTORIC	TRADE	SUMMARY			06 Oct 92	
<----------------LONG---------------->						<----------------SHORT---------------					
<----open---->	<----close---->			%		<----open---->		<----close---->			
SBRY	INDEXIA	20	40	55	363	0	INDEXIA	20	40	55	363 0
200686	194	091087		272	40.2	091087		272	030289		238 14
030289	238	151289		254	6.7	151289		254	080690		284 -10
080690	284	300891		364	28.2	300891		364	130392		380 -4
130392	380	200892		444	16.8	200892		444	061092		457 -2
			Total		91.9				Total		-3

Chart 3.9   Sainsbury daily close, October 1989–February 1993 (and INDEXIA 20, 40 and 55 trade summary)

I would then optimize my entry into the market by the use of the shorter-term oscillators that I will discuss in Chapter 4.

MOVING AVERAGE CONVERGENCE DIVERGENCE

The MACD uses two exponential moving averages – faster line and slower line. The faster line represents the mass mood of the market over a recent period, whereas the slower line measures the mood over a longer term. When the shorter-term line outruns the longer-term to the upside then the crowd is more bullish on the shorter term. On the other hand, when the shorter-term line falls behind the longer-term moving average then more selling pressure is coming into the market. When the MACD

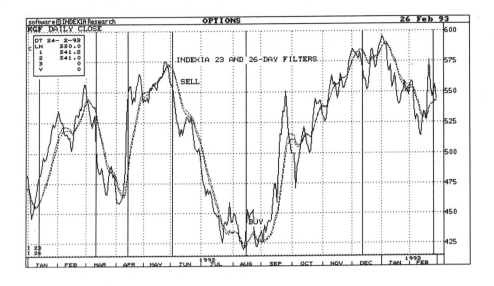

UK OPTIONS			HISTORIC TRADE SUMMARY			06 Oct 92		
<--------------LONG----------------->					<----------------SHORT----------------			
<-----open----->	<----close---->		%	<----open----->	<----close---->			
KGF	INDEXIA	23 26	0 1605 0		INDEXIA	23 26	0 1605 0	
050886	312	260986	307	-1.6	090686	412	050886	312	32
201086	317	160187	344	8.5	260986	307	201086	317	-3
200187	359	220187	349	-2.8	160187	344	200187	359	-4
020287	367	310387	399	8.7	220187	349	020287	367	-4
300487	421	050687	432	2.6	310387	399	300487	421	-5
110687	449	190687	426	-5.1	050687	432	110687	449	-3
040987	361	211087	332	-8.0	190687	426	040987	361	18
151287	254	280388	277	9.1	211087	332	151287	254	30
140488	290	150488	282	-2.8	280388	277	140488	290	-4
190488	290	200488	287	-1.0	150488	282	190488	290	-2
020688	294	170688	287	-2.4	200488	287	020688	294	-2
250788	283	270788	281	-0.7	170688	287	250788	283	1
080888	286	150888	278	-2.8	270788	281	080888	286	-1
170888	281	230888	274	-2.5	150888	278	170888	281	-1
200988	247	041188	242	-2.0	230888	274	200988	247	10
231188	264	061288	241	-8.7	041188	242	231188	264	-8
040189	238	210289	273	14.7	061288	241	040189	238	1
130489	273	310589	302	10.6	210289	273	130489	273	0
070789	312	170889	337	8.0	310589	302	070789	312	-3
081189	285	180190	289	1.4	170889	337	081189	285	18
270290	284	260490	276	-2.8	180190	289	270290	284	1
110590	290	020790	348	20.0	260490	276	110590	290	-4
260990	324	081190	375	15.7	020790	348	260990	324	7
170191	392	250191	370	-5.6	081190	375	170191	392	-4
040291	386	260491	492	27.5	250191	370	040291	386	-4
120791	505	050991	562	11.3	260491	492	120791	505	-2
011191	565	181191	538	-4.8	050991	562	011191	565	-0
140192	481	110392	503	4.6	181191	538	140192	481	11
130492	550	020692	554	0.7	110392	503	130492	550	-8
040892	449	061092	489	8.9	020692	554	040892	449	23
		Total		98.7			Total	86

Chart 3.10   KGF daily close, January 1992–February 1993 (and INDEXIA 23 and 26 trade summary)

line crosses the zero line, it means that the two averages being studied have crossed each other. However, this is no different than observing the moving averages themselves. So it is customary to draw a moving average on the MACD itself and buy/sell when this moving average/filter crosses the zero line.

Traditionally the MACD is measured using the exponential moving average, but with computerized techniques now available one can use simple, lagged or other moving averages to suit the type of trading you wish to carry out. At this stage of the book, I think it would be inappropriate to demonstrate the optimum moving averages for the MACD in relation to the FTSE. This is because, as previously stated, it depends on whether you are a short-term trader or a longer-term postion trader. Suffice to say that the example illustrated is again showing on average a 70 per cent success rate as it has done since 1988. However, I still prefer to use the MACD as a secondary tool.

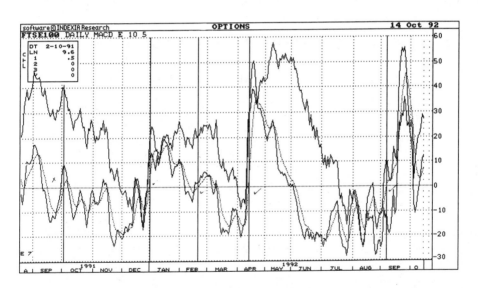

Chart 3.11   FTSE 100 daily close and MACD Exponential 10-day, 5-day, September 1991–October 1992

Chart 3.11 shows the MACD from September 1991 to 14 October 1992 with the daily close for the FTSE overlaid. Utilising the MACD and its filter as a buy signal only, during this period five signals were generated, of which four were correct. As far as the sell signal is concerned, I prefer to use a volume indicator (see Chapter 5).

Chart 3.12 shows the MACD from January to July 1991 with the FTSE daily close overlaid. Again utilizing the MACD filter as a buy signal, four

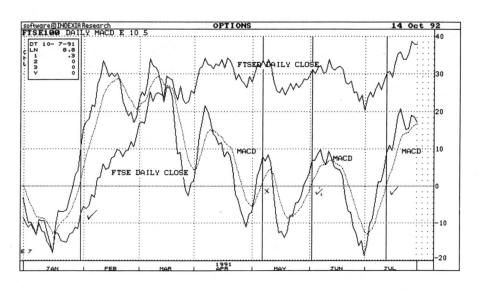

Chart 3.12   FTSE 100 daily close and MACD Exponential 10-day, 5-day, January–July 1991

signals were generated of which two if not three would have proved profitable.

INDICES

As far back as the turn of the century, Charles Dow, then editor of the *Wall Street Journal*, began studying the behaviour of prices of groups of shares and of the whole market. The measures he used to describe this behaviour were the first indices. In a nutshell, an index is a weighted average of the prices of a group of shares. It is a 'weighted' average because it is not just a straight arithmetic average of the prices of the shares in the group, but is a product of the prices multiplied by the number of shares issued in each company: in fact it is a measure of the 'market capitalization' of the group. However, since it can run into hundreds of millions, this figure is not used directly. Instead, it is compared with the figure at a certain arbitrary time, taken as the base.

The important point to note is that the actual value of an index is not at all important – its real significance lies in its value compared with yesterday's value, last week's value or last year's value. In short, indices enable us to keep track of trends in the market. Remember that an index is a good indicator of the combined price movements of a group of shares. It can happen, however, that an index will be kept going in one direction (eg upwards near the final phase of a bull market) by a small group of shares which are the 'market favourites'. At the same time, many shares in that group or in the whole market may have stopped advancing or may even be declining marginally. This is an indication that the market is turning and we need to detect it.

Advances and declines

Each day in the *Financial Times*, a table of 'rises and falls' shows how many securities rose, fell or remained unchanged in price during the previous trading session. Recording the net rises/falls is easy. Just subtract the number of different shares down (ie that declined in price) for the day from the number of shares up for the day. The result is the net rise/fall figure for insertion on to a worksheet. Work out the change from the previous day and record this figure in the movement column. It takes a little while manually, but most software programs now carry out the analysis autuomatically.

Chart 3.13 highlights the advance/decline for the FTSE 100 Index and the indicator provides a measure of whether the market as a whole is gaining or losing strength. If the market is rising but the advance/decline line is falling, then this indicates that the rally is running out of steam, and vice versa when the the market is falling and the advance/decline line is rising.

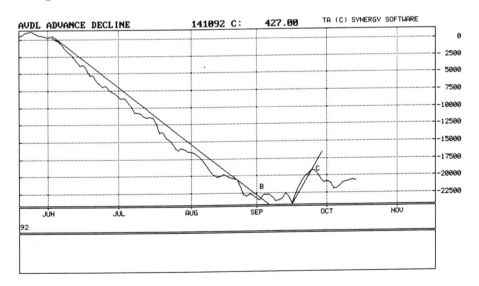

Chart 3.13   Advance/decline, June–October 1992

Chart 3.13 shows the advance/decline line from June 1992 to 14 October 1992. The downtrend for the advance/decline line can be seen to be broken at point B (3 September 1992) and then it started to rise. This indicator by itself should have put you on warning that buying strength was beginning to enter the market.

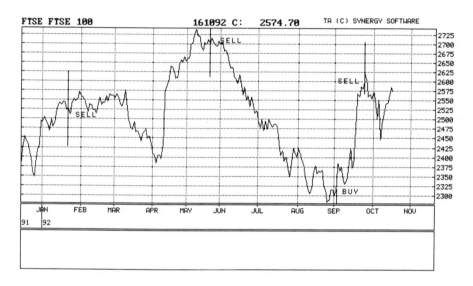

Chart 3.14   FTSE 100, December 1991–October 1992

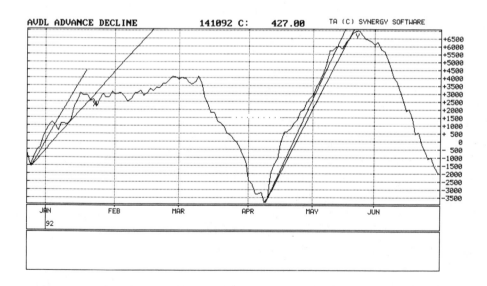

Chart 3.15   Advance/decline and fan lines, January–June 1992

Similarily at point C on the advance/decline line, the uptrend was broken and the date here was 24 September 1992. In fact this date was more or less the peak of this particular rally on the FTSE 100.

Chart 3.14 shows the corresponding buy and sell signals overlaid on the FTSE index to illustrate that divergence and break down of the trend was occurring between the advance/decline line and the FTSE daily closing chart.

At the commencement of a trend of the advance/decline line there is sometimes the possibility that the trend is not very well defined and, in this case, I favour using the fan lines – when the advance/decline line penetrates the second fan line then this is a strong signal to close your position in the market.

In Chart 3.15 I have marked the penetration points of the fan lines at point X (23 January 1992) and point Y (21 May 1992). One can then relate these dates to the FTSE daily close line chart (Chart 3.14) and see that these signals generated were really very good.

4

Short-term Oscillators

There are four oscillators which I use regularly and will now discuss in detail: the overbought/oversold indicator; momentum; the relative strength index (sometimes referred to as the rate of change indicator); and stochastics.

First, however, I must point out that these are only secondary indicators and should be used as confirmatory or warning signals within the major trend. Once you have established the major trend (See Chapters 1, 2 and 3) then the secondary short-term oscillators can be employed for fine tuning your entry and exit of that trend. Again, depending on the type of trading you wish to carry out, the optimum time period for these oscillators can be altered accordingly.

OVERBOUGHT/OVERSOLD INDICATOR

The OB/OS indicator shows the percentage by which a price is above (or below) the moving average selected. When the price reaches certain percentage levels away from the moving average, it is said to be either 'overbought' (if positive) or 'oversold' (if negative). When this happens, the chances are that the price will correct to rectify the situation.

Basically, what the indicator is telling us is that a point is reached where this greatly accelerated momentum of buying (overbought) or selling (oversold) can no longer be maintained and has to reverse. The OB/OS index is again a trend, and as long as the line keeps on rising even when in an overbought zone, no trend reversal need occur. It's when the moving total 'tops out' inside the overbought zone (or 'bottoms out' in the oversold zone) and begins to decline (advance) that a secondary reaction or, at best, a period of consolidation can be expected within a short time.

Chart 4.1 (lower) clearly shows that the OB/OS indicator was in an overbought zone with a reading of +8 towards the end of September 1992. It then started to move down out of this overbought zone, which was a warning signal that a correction on the FTSE was about to occur and, sure enough, the correction of 150 points in the FTSE took place a week later! It then entered into the oversold zone when the OB/OS

and this, coupled with the fact that the OB/OS was moving down from its overbought zone, was a strong indication that the market was due for a correction.

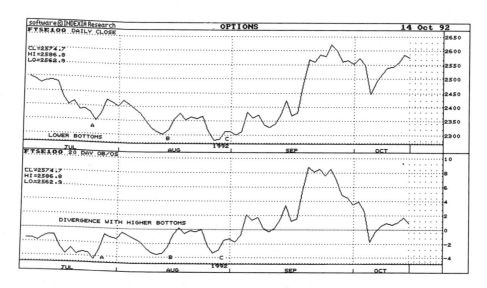

Chart 4.2   FTSE 100 daily close and 20-day OB/OS (divergence), July–October 1992

Chart 4.2 highlights the divergence factor in reverse. When the FTSE was making lower bottoms at the end of July and the middle of August, the 20-day OB/OS indicator was making higher bottoms and the FTSE finally began a new uptrend at the beginning of September 1992.

A further example of the OB/OS indicator working in the real market is illustrated in Chart 4.3. Historically, the OB/OS indicator shows an oversold reading at −5. If the OB/OS then starts to move out of this oversold zone – that is above −5 – then historically the odds are in your favour that the share price will rally. The chart covers the period from August 1991 to October 1992 and seven opportunities arose to buy call options on Marks & Spencer shares, out of which six trades would have resulted in a profit (an 85 per cent success rate).

The other important point to mention here is that one would not be purchasing further put options on a stock if the shares were in a primary downtrend but the OB/OS indicator was in the oversold zone, because a rally in the share price would probably be imminent. Instead, one would wait until the OB/OS indicator was overbought and the primary downtrend was still being confirmed.   Chart 4.4 shows a further example

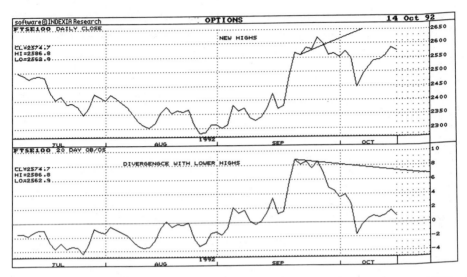

Chart 4.1 FTSE 100 daily close and 20-day OB/OS, July–October 1992

indicator stood at −2 and then started to move up out of this oversold zone, which was immediately followed by a correction on the upside by the FTSE daily close as well. Obviously the OB/OS indicator does not work as well as this all the time, but by using it with other primary indicators, your trading techniques will improve considerably.

Divergence

Another important aspect to watch out for when using these secondary indicators is divergence. This applies equally to all such indicators and a strong divergence factor on the relative strength indicator was highlighted in my weekly newsletter on 13 July 1987, just before the 1987 crash. The item stated:

> The market continues its uptrend reaching new peaks yet again! However, the rate of change indicator is a little disturbing due to divergence factors compared to the FTSE chart. Whereas the FTSE is finding new peaks, the rate of change indicator is *not* finding new peaks and this divergence usually indicates a bearish situation is about to occur. . . .The market will need careful monitoring over the forthcom ing weeks.

Turning to more recent events, Chart 4.1 for the FTSE 100 also highlight period of divergence with the FTSE making higher tops from the mid to the end of September 1992, whereas the OB/OS was making lower t

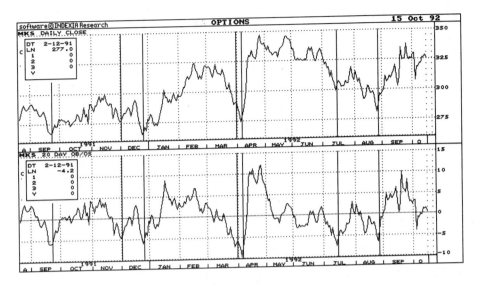

Chart 4.3 Marks and Spencer daily close and 20-day OB/OS, August 1991–October 1992

of buying opportunities (in Cable and Wireless) when the 20-day OB/OS was oversold. Again a −5 reading proved to be the critical area.

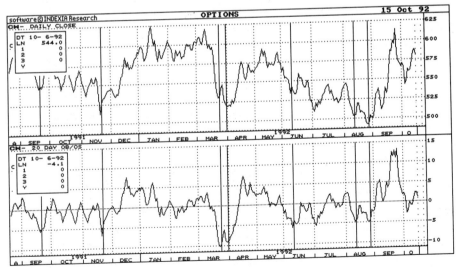

Chart 4.4 Cable and Wireless daily close and 20-day OB/OS, August 1991–October 1992

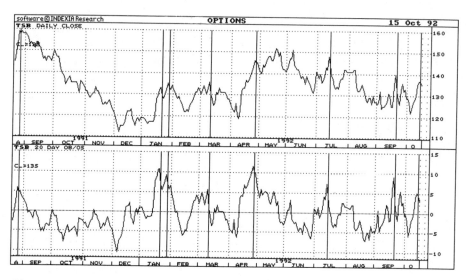

Chart 4.5   TSB daily close and 20-day OB/OS, August 1991–October 1992

In Chart 4.5 we are using the OB/OS indicator to tell us when shares are overbought and likely to reverse downwards. Historically with TSB, an overbought reading occurs at +5, and when the OB/OS starts to move down from this overbought zone then there is a good chance that the share price will also correct. During the period from August 1991 to October 1992 there were seven opportunities to trade put positions and five of these would have been correct, while the last trade has yet to be proven.

Chart 4.6 shows the hourly FTSE 100 and the 20-hour OB/OS. When the OB/OS gives an oversold reading of −2 or more and then moves back up through the −2 oversold level, one takes a long position in the market. The important concept here is that the OB/OS must move back up through the −2 level before a trade is activated, and the overall primary trend for the daily FTSE must be long as well. In this example, the two trades produced excellent results.

Chart 4.7 illustrates the daily close for the Dow Jones and the 20-day OB/OS for the period from late-August 1991 to 15 October 1992. Historically, when the OB/OS indicator reaches a reading of −2 or more and then starts to move up then the chances are that the Dow will rally from its oversold position. Chart 4.8 highlights the same indicator. For the period from January to July 1991 there were five opportunities to trade the Dow and all proved to be correct (with three of these trades involving sustained rallies). Similarly, from October 1991 to October 1992 there were

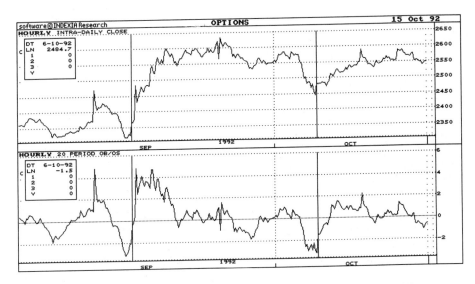

Chart 4.6 FTSE 100 hourly intra-daily close and 20-day OB/OS, September–October 1992

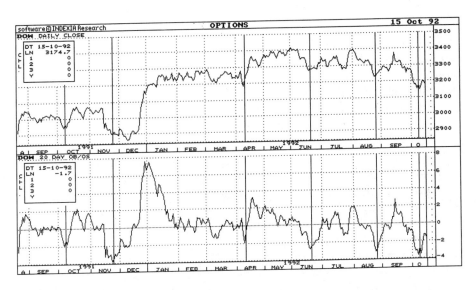

Chart 4.7 Dow Jones daily close and 20-day OB/OS, August 1991–October 1992

six opportunities to trade long of the Dow and four have proved to be correct, with the outcome of last trade still awaited.

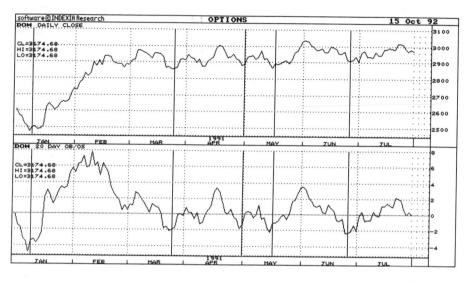

Chart 4.8   Dow Jones daily close and 20-day OB/OS, January–July 1991

MOMENTUM

Momentum measures the *rate of change* of prices as opposed to the actual price levels themselves. It is measured over a fixed time interval, usually 10 or 20 days. In order to construct the 10-day momentum line, one subtracts the closing price 10 days ago from the most recent closing price. The line then oscillates above and below the zero line showing the times of positive and negative price velocity.

A positive, rising momentum indicates that the price trend is not only rising (velocity increasing) but that it is also accelerating. This is bullish and indicates that the price is in a strong uptrend. A falling momentum in the positive area indicates that the price trend is still rising but that it is decelerating. It is during this phase that momentum warns us that prices are ready to fall.

Chart 4.9 clearly demonstrates this and also confirms the usefulness of combining the OB/OS indicator with the momentum indicator. Not only did we have divergence from the OB/OS plus a move away from the overbought zone with a previous reading of +8, but the momentum indicator was also moving down in the positive area at the end of September, warning us that prices were about to fall and, sure enough, that is exactly what happened. The last plots indicate a move into negative territory. A negative falling momentum value indicates that the price trend is not only falling (velocity increasing in the opposite direction) but that it is also accelerating downwards. This is bearish and indicates that

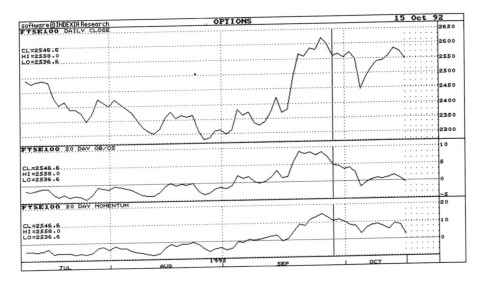

Chart 4.9 FTSE 100 daily close, 20-day OB/OS and 20-day momentum, July–October 1992

the price is in a strong downtrend. This was clearly demonstrated by the FTSE 100 Index at the end of May and the beginning of June 1992.

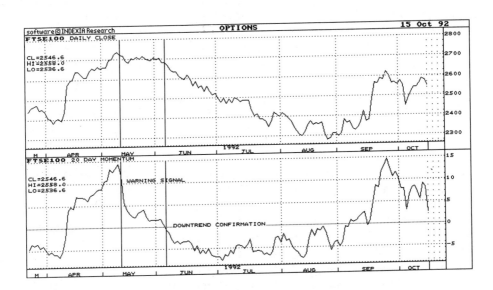

Chart 4.10 FTSE 100 daily close and 20-day momentum, March–October 1992

Chart 4.10 highlights the use of 20-day momentum. It gave ample warning of the downtrend to come and then, once the indicator had moved down through the zero line, provided a clear indication that a new downtrend was in existence. A rising momentum in the negative area indicates that the price trend is still falling but that it is decelerating. It is during this phase that momentum warns us that prices are ready to rise.

In simple terms, the formula for momentum is $M = V - V_x$, where V is the latest closing price and V_x is the closing price a specified number of days ago. As with moving averages, the shorter the time period selected, the more sensitive the indicator.

When the momentum line moves below the zero line, the latest 20-day (ie 20-day period selected) closing price is now under the closing of 20 days ago and, as the momentum line continues to drop further, the downtrend is gaining momentum. Only when the downtrend movement ceases and begins to reverse does the investor know that the downtrend is decelerating. Again, positive divergence should also be taken into consideration when assessing the likelihood of the end of a downtrend. This is clearly illustrated with the FTSE 100 at the end of August 1992, when the Index was making lower bottoms but 20-day momentum was making higher bottoms.

RELATIVE STRENGTH INDEX

The relative strength index (RSI), sometimes referred to as the rate of change indicator, is a measure of momentum and not the measure of relative strength between two entities. The RSI tells us when a stock or index is overbought or oversold – in other words, when a move is accelerating or slowing down. The RSI is measured between zero and 100 and, when this indicator is below 25, the underlying index or stock is said to be oversold, whereas a reading above 75 means it is overbought.

However, one should be very careful about reading too much into these overbought and oversold criteria. In a strongly trending bull market I have often noticed that although the RSI shows a reading of 75+ it has still not turned down and, in fact, can quite often reach 85+. The difference in a rising market between an RSI reading of 75 and one of 90 can often be 150 index points. So, just because the RSI is in the overbought zone, it does not necessarily mean that a correction is imminent and, similarly, when the index is oversold. In fact the main use of the RSI that I personally find most rewarding is that of divergence.

Chart 4.11 illustrates this with the 14-day RSI for the FTSE 100 Index. You can see that the RSI was giving an overbought reading in the middle of February 1991 at point A (an RSI of 78) – the Index at this stage stood at 2318. Although the RSI did take a correction, the market continued to climb to the next level of 2459 where the RSI was *not* in divergence and

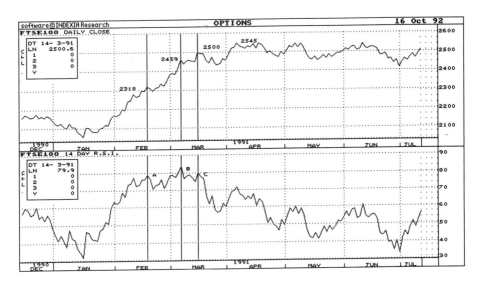

Chart 4.11 FTSE 100 daily close and 14-day RSI, December 1990–July 1991

again was showing an overbought reading of 84. It is only at this stage (with the FTSE continuing to rise to 2500) that the RSI failed to make a new high – ie, divergence had now crept in. It is at this point that the trader should be aware that the rise in the market was about to come to an end. Indeed, shortly afterwards at 2545 the market started to turn sideways and entered a quite lengthy period of consolidation.

As previously stated, just because the RSI is overbought in itself, this does not necessarily mean that the bull run of the stock or index has come to an end. The perception of divergence is usually a better measure of the market direction than the RSI reading itself. Another example of divergence occurs in reverse (see Chart 4.12) when the RSI for the FTSE was oversold but making higher lows at points A, B and C, whereas the FTSE daily close was making lower lows. Again this was indicative that the market's downtrend was about to terminate. It is also important to use the trend indicators on your daily files in conjuction with the RSI.

In Chart 4.13 for the Dow I have highlighted the buy signals using only an historic break out of the oversold reading. However, although five out of the last seven signals were correct, I personally would advise against trading in this manner. As can be clearly seen in November 1991 when the short-term downtrend was still in existence, the two signals generated by the RSI were false – so don't buck the trend! Only once the downtrend has been broken should you consider the trade. It is also important to remember that the RSI is a *secondary* indicator.

Chart 4.14 for Boots shows an historical overbought reading for the RSI

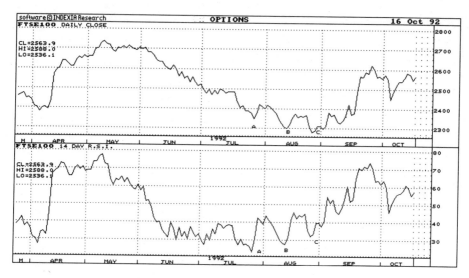

Chart 4.12   FTSE 100 daily close and 14-day RSI, March–October 1992

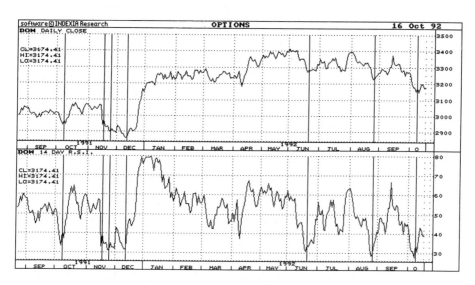

Chart 4.13   Dow Jones daily close and 14-day RSI, September 1991–October 1992

at 70+ which has proved successful. But again, notice the divergence towards the end of February 1992 when the daily close for Boots was making new highs but the RSI failed to do so. This highlighted the negative divergence, and eventually the share price moved rapidly

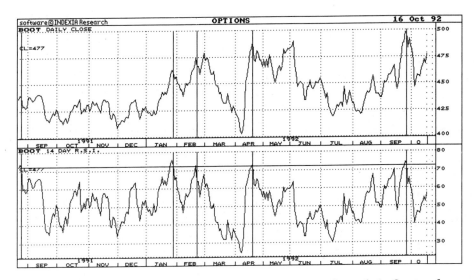

Chart 4.14 Boots daily close and 14-day RSI (overbought), September 1991–October 1992

southwards from the beginning of March 1992. Chart 4.15, also for Boots shows an historically oversold zone at an RSI reading of 33, with the corresponding buy signals overlaid on the daily close chart for the period from September 1991 to October 1992.

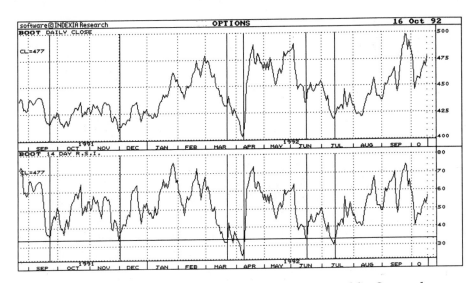

Chart 4.15 Boots daily close and 14-day RSI (oversold), September 1991–October 1992

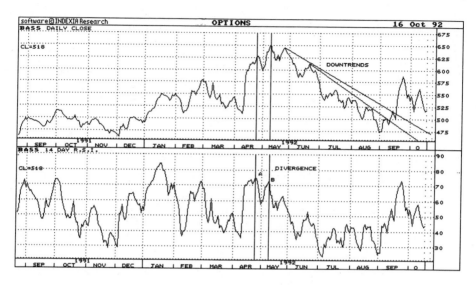

Chart 4.16   BASS daily close and 14-day RSI, September1991–October 1992

Chart 4.16 for Bass highlights the downtrend in existence from June 1992. Warning of this impending downtrend was given by the divergence occurring at points A and B where the RSI was making lower tops but the daily close for Bass was still making higher tops.

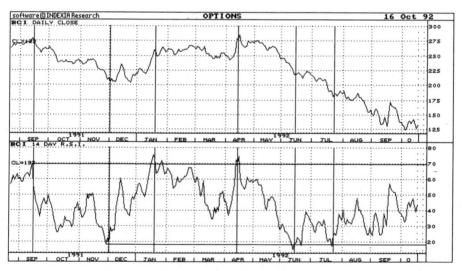

Chart 4.17   Blue Circle daily close and 14-day RSI, September 1991–October 1992

Chart 4.17 for Blue Circle also shows the historic overbought and oversold zones. The importance of not bucking the trend when using this secondary indicator is clearly highlighted: with the downtrend in existence from May 1992 and although the RSI was showing an historic oversold reading in June and July 1992, these signals should have been ignored until the downtrend had been broken and a new uptrend established.

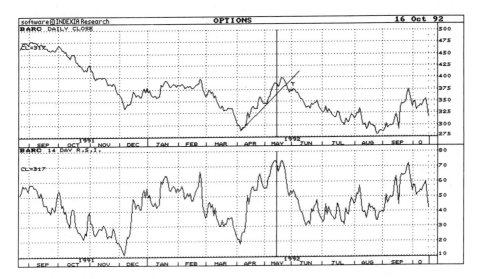

Chart 4.18   Barclays daily close and 14-day RSI, September 1991–October 1992

Similarly, Chart 4.18 for Barclays shows that the RSI was giving an overbought reading of 75 in the middle of May 1992, but the uptrend on the daily close chart for Barclays was still in existence. Although the RSI started to move down from its overbought reading, no action should have been taken until the uptrend was broken at point T.

STOCHASTICS

Stochastic indicators are based on the premise that closing prices tend to accumulate near tops of each period's trading range during price uptrends and at the bottom during price downtrends. Simply speaking, a stochastic is an indicator of momentum and the principle behind the basic stochastic curve is that as price decreases then lows tend to be near the lower end of the range and vice versa as prices increase. The stochastic curve is calculated on a moving basis using the following formula:

$$\frac{\text{latest price} - \text{period low}}{\text{period high} - \text{period low}}$$

and is plotted in a range of zero to 100.

The stochastic curve comes in a regular and slow form. Regular or pure stochastics consists of two lines: a K or solid line and a percentage D or dotted line. The slow is a smooth version of the regular where the K on the slow is the same as the percentage D on the regular. As with other indicators, the degree of measurement depending on whether you are trading short term, medium or long term can be altered according to your trading requirements.

For the short-term measure, a moving period of 14 days and a smoothing period of three days is often used or, alternatively, a 21-day moving period and a three-day smoothing period. As with the RSI, divergence is also a feature of stochastics but with more pronounced areas of consolidation this is often harder to identify. After a strong rise or fall, prices do tend to consolidate. If, during this consolidation, prices close away from the extremes, the stochastic curve will start to move in the opposite direction, indicating an imminent price reversal. As with all oscillators, stochastics indicate overbought and oversold areas as well.

Since raw stochastics relates the current price to its relative position compared to the range of the past 14 days, the readings which vary from zero to 100 make interpretation of K and D much easier. Basically, buy signals are given when K rises above D, with sell signals generated by K moving below D, but again remembering not to buck the trend and also bearing in mind that this indicator is a secondary one. I have found stochastics particularly useful when trading both the FTSE 100 Index and the sterling/dollar rate.

Chart 4.19 highlights the daily close for the FTSE 100 with a major sell occurring towards the end of March 1991. However, at this pont the three-day slow stochastic was giving an oversold reading and moving up. It is more prudent to wait until the stochastic is at least moving down from an overbought reading before going short of the market, and this occurred at the beginning of April when the FTSE 100 stood at 2529 as opposed to 2440 – a difference of 89 points!

Chart 4.20 (upper) highlights a major sell for sterling at point A. However, the three-day slow stochastic was giving a very oversold reading at this level, so again it was necessary to wait until (a) the stochastic moved back up into its overbought zone and then (b) started to move down again. This it did and the sell came into place at point B, which proved to be worth five cents more – a considerable saving.

Chart 4.21 (upper) confirms that the FTSE 100 was in a new uptrend from the beginning of September 1992. One could then optimise entry into the market by use of the slow stochastic three-day period. When the stochastic gives a reading of less than 20 and then starts to move up, while

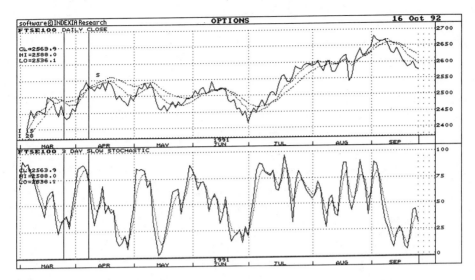

Chart 4.19 FTSE 100 daily close and three-day slow stochastic, March–September 1991

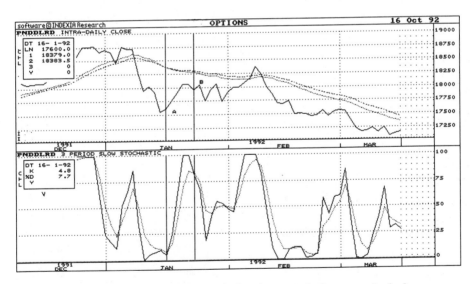

Chart 4.20 Sterling/dollar intra-daily close and three-period slow stochastic, December 1991–March 1992

the major uptrend is in place, then the resulting signals prove to be accurate. I am not saying that you just rely on the stochastic to trade the market, but by the use of your other indicators combined with these

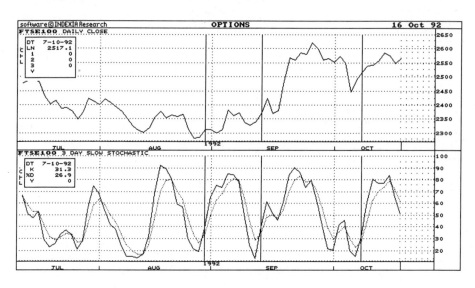

Chart 4.21   FTSE 100 daily close and three-day slow stochastic, July–October 1992

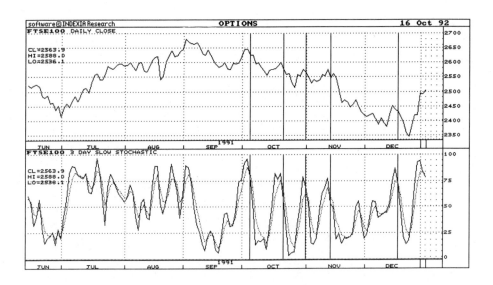

Chart 4.22   FTSE 100 daily close and three-day slow stochastic, June–December 1991

secondary indicators including the stochastic, the risk/reward scenario is greatly enhanced.

Finally, in Chart 4.22, the FTSE 100 is in a clear downtrend from the beginning of October 1991. By using the three-day slow stochastic, which is giving a reading of 75+ in the overbought zone and starting to move down, one can improve market entry accuracy when taking up short positions.

5

FTSE Trend Setter

Over the last eight years I have studied technical analysis in some depth, and early on I believed that moving averages were the answer to finding a seat in wonderland. Unfortunately I soon discovered that as soon as markets stop trending then these moving averages fail to work and, indeed, the term 'whiplash' soon became prominent in my vocabulary. After commencing with a simple BBC computer and a simple moving average program, I then stepped up my exposure to technical analysis, still confident that I was on the right track, and I bought a number of so-called computerized technical analysis programs. However, after much trial and error and costly mistakes in the market I still could not find a system that lived up to its promises.

At first I tried to look at all stocks plus a number of indices but soon found that each stock, let alone the indices, behaves in a unique way and certain indicators that work for a particular stock or index do not work for another. So I set about concentrating my efforts on the FTSE 100 Index and tried and tested various mathematical formulae and calculus to endeavour to arrive at a computerized trading system that did not necessarily get you in at the bottom or out at the top of the market, but produced consistently good results with relatively few trades. Thus I developed the FTSE Trend Setter program.

However, as previously mentioned, it is not always the system that is wrong: it can be the trader who simply does not obey the rules applicable to that particular system. Jumping in too early, in anticipation of that long-awaited, elusive signal or perhaps getting out too early on what initially appeared to be the start of new trend downwards but in fact was only a correction in the market.

The Trend Setter program, is not an advisory system, telling you when to buy or sell – it merely highlights the major strengths and weaknesses in the market and, between these areas, it highlights minor strengths and weaknesses. In addition, it also helps to locate important support and resistance levels according to the theories of W.D. Gann and the Fibonacci retracement levels. Imagine your confidence if a level of major strength is signalled in the market and this happens to be the same level as a G2 (Gann level) and/or a 50 per cent Fibonacci retracement level as well!

SYSTEM PRINCIPLES

It is my belief that there is order in the market-place and this can be used to predict future market movements. Over the last six months I have therefore teamed up with a leading programmer from an international bank and you will now be able to see the results that have been achieved by the FTSE Trend Setter program (CATS). Examples of how you can use Trend Setter will be discussed later on in this chapter (course details available on request).

First of all you must have read my book and have understood the basic concepts behind trading the FTSE Index, whether it be through the options or futures markets. Imagine that we are at the beginning of September 1992 and over the last three months you have been busily updating your database every day with the FTSE high, low, close, volume and so on, but still no major signal of strength has appeared on your screen. However, you are feeling quite pleased with yourself, since you were able to pick up the turning point in the market when the Trend Setter signalled a level of major weakness at the beginning of June 1992 ahead of a fall of over 300 points! You are convinced that the market should have turned upwards by now and of course, being a disciplined trader, you continue to wait, but by this time you are becoming a little despondent and impatient and you are beginning to wonder how long this bear market is going to continue. You've read reports that the FTSE is now going to drop to the 2220 level, if not the 1800 level, and then, all of a sudden, the system signals that there has been a change in the instinct of the herd and major strength has arrived in the market once again.

I am not going to reveal all the secrets of the system to you, but I will tell you, at least, that volume has a very important role to play. Once you have put the trades in place you must then decide when to consolidate your position, and this again is highlighted in the program. The charts for the period from August 1992 to October 1992 show that major strength appeared in the market early in September and a period of consolidation occurred in early-October at a level of 2601. This gave you ample opportunities to lock in a good position and await further instructions (20/10/92). But it is important to state that although you have taken and consolidated your position, major weakness has not yet appeared again and all you are doing at this stage is taking a strategic rest and considering your next strategy.

Don't forget it is important to know when *not* to trade as well as knowing when to enter and exit the market. Since we closed out the long trade at 2553, the market has fallen by just over 100 points and then made it all up again – not exactly ideal conditions for going long or short! The system was designed to pick up major trends in the market that will be sustained, but also enables you to lock in considerable profits while at the same time removing the elements of fear and greed by leaving that little bit extra for the other trader.

PYRAMIDING THE FTSE

Although I have now written three books on technical analysis and traded options, I am conscious that the real market is very different to the theoretical market-place. It is for this reason that I thought it would be effective to produce a system that highlights the major strengths and weaknesses in the market and which, in turn, enables you to pyramid the FTSE within these parameters.

For example, in 1992 during the bull movement from September to December, there were eight opportunities to pyramid the FTSE, which resulted in a further increment of 749 points. Again, during the period of major weakness from June to late-August there were three opportunities to pyramid the FTSE on the way down, which resulted in a further gain to the portfolio of 168 points.

I am not saying that this system is infallible; but it has worked out the risk–reward of pyramiding and only allows this type of signal to occur on a limited number of occasions. The whole purpose of Trend Setter is to position trade. In other words, entering the market when a confirmatory uptrend is in place and exiting from this trade before a new major downtrend exists and wipes all the gains away. It will then allow you to enter the market on the downside before the onslaught has set in. I have spent many months testing this system and have actually traded it successfully. I am satisfied that it is accurate enough to promote.

I could go on explaining the system *ad infinitum* but a picture paints a thousand words and this is why I have included a number of charts in the remainder of this chapter. But remember, these latest signals were determined in 1990–91 and absolutely no modifications or variations to the system have been carried out since 1991. Once the order and methodology had been established then the FTSE 100 Index was put to the test.

Of course, not all signals are going to be absolutely spot on, and in some cases there will be a pull back. On some occasions they will be early but on others slightly later; but the important message is that if the signal is wrong the system will pull you out of the position quickly with limited downside to your portfolio. It will not leave you in a position of wondering what to do next.

THE SYSTEM IN OPERATION

Table 5.1 highlights the major long positions opened and closed since November 1990. (Further backdated historical trades can be seen on the Trend Setter program itself, and if you wish to receive further information on this system please write to me at Suite C, 6 Cromwell Crescent, London, SW5 9QN.) Charts 5.1–5.6 highlight the open and close

Table 5.1 Major long positions, November 1990–October 1992

Date (position open)	FTSE	Date (position close)	FTSE	Pull down*	Gain/(loss)
20/11/90	2095	17/12/90	2157	–	62
30/01/91	2113	15/03/91	2494	–	381
15/07/91	2532	10/09/91	2630	–	98
09/01/92	2493	21/01/92	2543	26	50
23/04/92	2600	27/05/92	2698	–	98
11/09/92	2340	25/09/92	2601	–	261
20/10/92	2617	09/12/92	2750	–	133

*maximum potential loss while trade still open

positions for these trades. (It would not be appropriate to discuss trading techniques for this system here, but I have written a book on such techniques which involves options and futures and covered call writing.

As mentioned earlier, Trend Setter also allows you to pyramid while the major trend is still in place. Table 5.2 highlights the trades that would have been carried out while the major long positions from 11 September and 20 October 1992 were still being held during 1992/3 and before any major sell signal had been given (see Charts 5.2 and 5.3).

This type of pyramid trading is obviously more suitable to the futures market but, when trading these markets, tread very carefully and perhaps only open one contract to start with, until you have built up your confidence to trade the system.

If we now turn to shorting the market following Trend Setter signals, equally impressive results have been obtained over the last six years. Charts 5.4–5.6 highlight the trades for major short positions from 1989 to February 1993.

As with the long positions, Trend Setter also highlights the trades that can be carried out for pyramiding the market on the downside, as long as the major short position is still in place (see Charts 5.6–5.8)

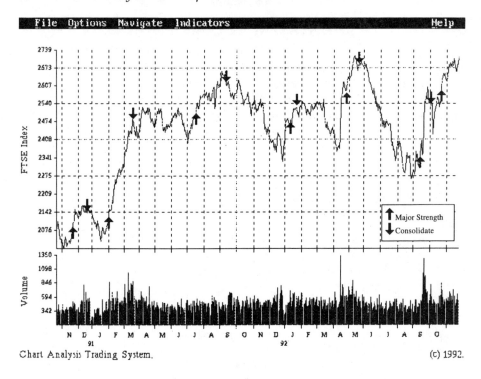

Chart Analysis Trading System.   (c) 1992.

Chart 5.1   FTSE 100 major strengths (opening positions) plus consolidations (closing positions)

Table 5.2   Trades between 17 September 1992 and 1 February 1993

Date (position open)	FTSE	Date (position closed)	FTSE	Gain/(loss)
17/09/92	2485	28/09/92	2573	88
17/09/92	2483	28/09/92	2560	77
07/10/92	2517	09/12/92	2750	233
12/10/92	2557	09/12/92	2750	193
30/10/92	2658	09/11/92	2695	37
10/11/92	2718	13/11/92	2706	(12)
26/11/92	2736	03/12/92	2758	22
14/12/92	2721	30/12/92	2832	111
22/01/93	2781	04/02/93	2865	84
01/02/93	2851	04/02/93	2865	14

Total points = 847!

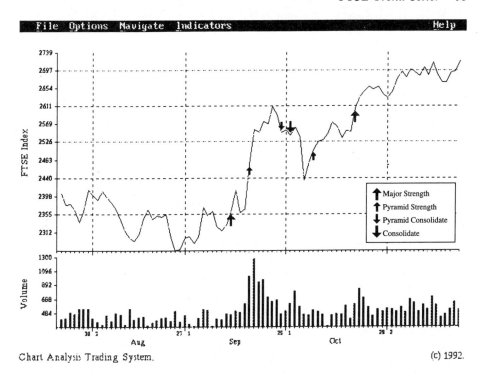

Chart Analysis Trading System.   (c) 1992.

Chart 5.2

THE IMPORTANCE OF VOLUME

As volume plays a critical role in the establishment of the rules for the Trend Setter program, I thought it would be prudent to discuss some key points regarding volume. Volume tells us the amount of activity that is taking place in the market; in other words it is a measure of supply and demand for shares. Volume should be studied in relation to the trend of the market: rising Volume during an uptrend is confirmation that the trend is still intact and basically a bullish forecast is made when prices and volume agree in direction.

However, one should be careful of very sudden, sharp rises in volume which usually cannot be sustained in the short term, and this is where profit taking usually sets in. Typical examples of this situation occurred when we joined the Exchange Rate Mechanism in October 1990 and left it again in September 1992.

Similarly, a sharp increase in volume was recorded in April 1992 when the Conservatives were surprisingly elected to form the next government: as depicted in Chart 5.7, a few days later this level of volume could not be maintained and a modest correction of approximately 75 points set in, before the uptrend gathered pace once again.

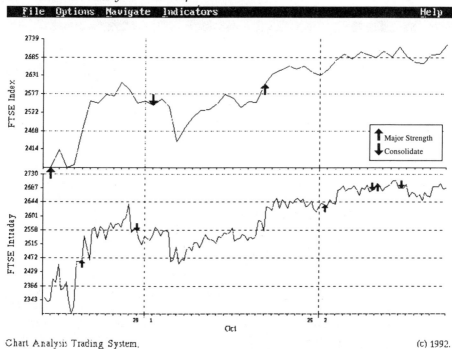

Chart 5.3   FTSE 100 daily close with intraday

Chart 5.4   FTSE 100 major weaknesses (opening positions) plus consolidations (closing positions)

Chart 5.5 FTSE 100 major weaknesses and consolidation

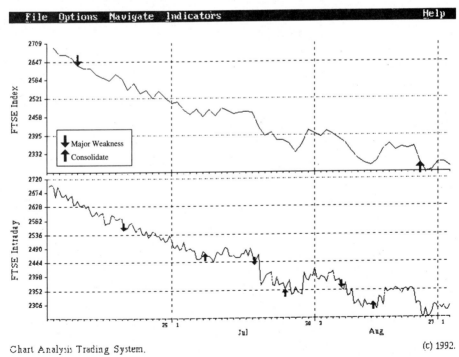

Chart 5.6

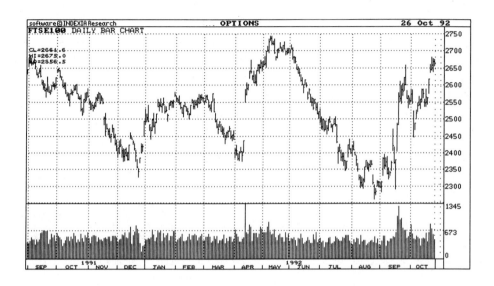

Chart 5.7   FTSE 100 daily bar chart, July 1990–January 1991

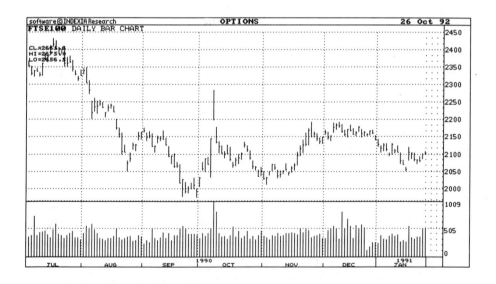

Chart 5.8   FTSE 100 daily bar chart, September 1991–October 1992

As regards volume in relation to gaps, when a breakaway gap is accompanied by increased volume this often signals the commencement of a new uptrend in the market. The opposite to this occurs at the end of the rising market when an exhaustion gap appears, accompanied by heavy volume.

Gaps

A gap is defined as a day's trading which takes place at a price level which, at no point, touches the range of the previous day's trading. On a daily bar chart, a gap will appear between the first day's trading and the second. Although arbitrage can cause a gap, for our purposes it is usually caused by the lack of sellers overnight. The next day the price opens higher or sometimes lower if there is a lack of buyers.

There are four types of gap:

1. Common
2. Breakaway
3. Runaway
4. Exhaustion

Breakaway gap

A breakaway gap is more important than the common gap which most chartists tend to ignore. It also only occurs in thinly traded markets. The breakaway gap often signals the commencement of a strong market move and often occurs on heavy volume, breaking away from a congestion area.

Runaway gap

After prices have been moving ahead for some time, usually in the middle of the move, another runaway gap (sometimes known as a measuring gap) appears.

In this instance, volume is usually moderate and, if the market is still trending upwards, this gap is a sign of continued strength in the market. It is often referred to as the measuring gap simply because it usually occurs at the half-way point in the trend.

Exhaustion gap

Here the supply of sellers is exhausted and the remaining buyers get their shares at a substantially higher price, hence the gap. The exhaustion gap appears towards the end of the market move and is usually accompanied by heavy volume. The final pattern that should be noted is the island reversal. This usually occurs after the exhaustion gap, when prices trade in a fairly narrow range for a couple of days and then gap down, leaving the price curve looking like an island surrounded by space, hence the name.

6

The INDEXIA II Plus System

INDEXIA Research was formed in 1983 with the specific aim of computerising technical analysis. It's first program, the INDEXIA Research Market Analyser was a pioneering system. Since then the company has progressed with the times and is now regarded as a leader in its field. The founders of INDEXIA Research are technical analysts themselves, with many years trading experience, so they know how to provide creative solutions to technical analysis problems.

Their latest product, INDEXIA II Plus, succeeds the INDEXIA II system. When it was released a few years ago, INDEXIA II was recognized as a new generation of technical analysis software. It is still used by professional and amateur analysts alike, although most of these have now moved to the more powerful INDEXIA II Plus. With INDEXIA II Plus, the company has tried to incorporate every technique that a technical analyst could require – for example, Gann angles and retracements, Fibonacci fan lines and arcs, wave charts, Japanese candlesticks, equivolume, and least squares regressions. INDEXIA II Plus is exceptionally strong in a number of areas – in particular ease of use, point and figure charts, trend line tools, proprietary indicators and moving averages (especially the INDEXIA filters).

EASY TO USE

With INDEXIA II Plus, INDEXIA Research has achieved ease of use, in spite of the vast array of charts and tools. Importantly for the analyst, the operation of one tool does not interfere with the next, making the system a pleasure to use. The trend line facility in the point and figure is a case in point – trend lines are automatically positioned at 45 degrees – a real time saver. Of course, if you prefer, you may move the lines to any angle.

Decisions concerning positioning of trend lines or drawing moving averages are left to the user to make when the chart is on the screen. INDEXIA avoids the practice of forcing the user through a series of menus in order to draw something as simple as a moving average or a trend line. With a chart on the screen, a simple command like 'M13' draws a 13-day moving average or 'T' calls up the trend line arrow which follows the line automatically so that positioning is achieved with the minimum delay. Even parallel lines are drawn automatically, which can be cleared if not required.

POINT AND FIGURE CHARTS

INDEXIA Research is strong on point and figure charting and the INDEXIA II Plus system offers a number of unique features. For example, it allows the user to draw point and figure charts based on the close price, or alternatively based on the high and low, thus covering two important schools of thought. It allows point and figure charts to be drawn on arithmetic as well as log scales, a unique feature which produces some very interesting results. Furthermore, it will even count vertical and horizontal price targets automatically. The count facility is especially useful on log scaled charts as manual counting is nigh impossible.

Chart 6.1 of the FTSE 100 Index shows the different patterns produced when point and figure charts are drawn on arithmetic and log scales using close only as well as high and low.

Chart A is an arithmetic scale point and figure based on close only. Chart B is an arithmetic scale point and figure based on high and low. Notice that the consolidation areas are wider when the high and low is used. This makes it easier to recognise patterns and in many cases it makes the horizontal counts more reliable. Chart C is a log scale point and figure based on close only, while Chart D is a log scale point and figure based on high and low. The box size on log scale charts is entered as a percentage and so the number of points per box varies as the price or index value varies. In the example shown, a 1 per cent box size is used. This represents a box size of approximately 27 points near the top and 17 points near the bottom of the chart. Once again, the high/low chart produces wider consolidation patterns.

The benefit of the wider patterns is shown in Charts 6.2 and 6.3 – two point and figure charts of Fisons. Chart 6.2 is a 5 × 3* based on the close, while Chart 6.3 is a 5 × 3 based on the high and low. The inverse fulcrum† top is wider on the high/low chart and in fact produces a more accurate horizontal downside count. It is also interesting to note that the high/low

---

* 5 means 5 box, ie the price has to advance 5 pence before a box with an 'X' is drawn on the chart. 3 means 3 box reversal, ie before a '0' is plotted the price has to decline by 15 pence (5 × 3).
† a fulcrum is a well defined congestion area, usually occurring after a significant advance or decline.

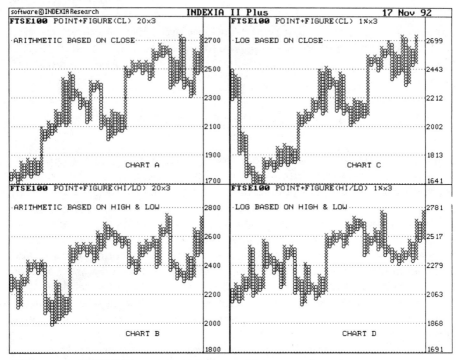

Chart 6.1 INDEXIA point and figure charts

Chart 6.2 Fisons 5 × 3 point and figure, based on close

chart has built a fulcrum or saucer bottom, whereas the close only chart exhibits a simple upside break out.

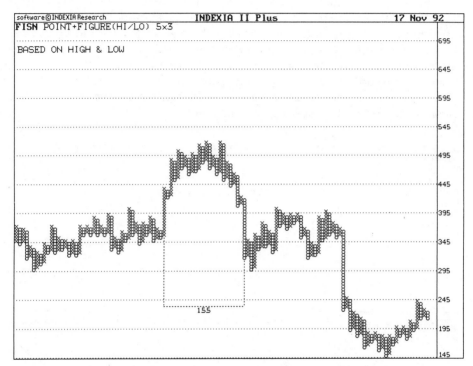

Chart 6.3 Fisons 5 × 3 point and figure, based on high/low

PROPRIETARY TECHNICAL INDICATORS

INDEXIA II Plus provides the whole spectrum of technical tools and charts. Its speed and versatility allows users to become expert and develop complete confidence in their ability to read the market.

In addition to having all the known techniques, INDEXIA II Plus has a number of proprietary charts and tools, like the INDEXIA filters, which are covered in more detail in the following pages. While they are a small part of the overall trading system, they are particularly useful, in that like moving averages they are objective, trend following indicators.

Another technical indicator which has found popularity is INDEXIA's Market Tracker – a fixed scale overbought/oversold oscillator. Its merit lies not in its ability to predict changes of trend, but rather its ability to clearly show danger areas. Chart 6.4 shows the FTSE 100 Index with a 21-day

Market Tracker below. The Market Tracker ranges between −100 and +100 and attempts to assign probabilities to the price reversals. In the −80 to −100 area, there is a high probability of the price turning up. Provided the indicator continues to move down or even levels out, the status quo should be maintained. The trader, however, should be aware that a turning point is imminent and possible short positions should be closed. It is customary to begin opening long positions once the indicator starts moving up again. In the +80 to +100 area there is a high probability of the price turning down. Once again the same rules apply. Certainly, no new longs should be opened at these levels. In fact, wary traders may start closing out some of their longs at this stage.

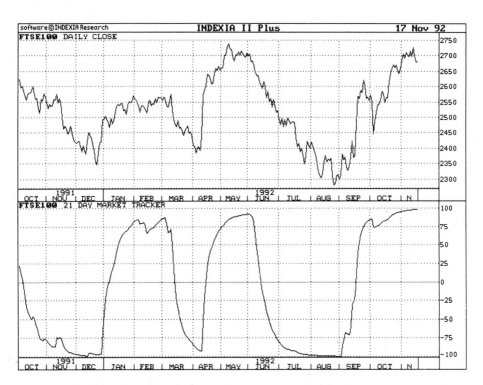

Chart 6.4 FTSE 100 daily close and Market Tracker, October 1991–November 1992

THE INDEXIA FILTERS

The INDEXIA filters look like moving averages, they are shaped and trend like moving averages, but they are much more efficient as the following

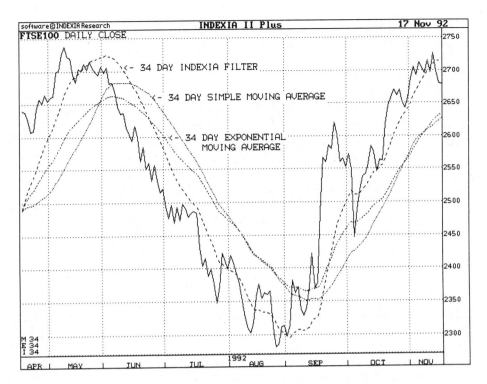

software ⓒ INDEXIA Research   **INDEXIA II Plus**   **17 Nov 92**

FTSE100 DAILY CLOSE

< - 34 DAY INDEXIA FILTER

< - 34 DAY SIMPLE MOVING AVERAGE

< - 34 DAY EXPONENTIAL MOVING AVERAGE

Chart 6.5   FTSE 100 daily close, INDEXIA filter and moving averages, April–November 1992

charts will demonstrate. They follow the price action so closely, that during strong up and downtrends they run through the middle of the price action. It is for this reason that INDEXIA filters should be used in pairs or threes. Compare the price actions of the same period (34-day) simple, exponential and INDEXIA filters in Chart 6.5.

Imposing a signal delay

One of the most effective ways of avoiding whipsaws is to impose a signal delay. This simply means waiting for a specific period for the signal to be confirmed – a sort of cooling-off period. It does often lead to buying at a higher price and selling at a lower price, but it is better to be late and correct than early and wrong.

This method does not eliminate all whipsaws, but it is more effective than some other whipsaw avoiding techniques. Knowing when and how many days or weeks delay to impose requires some trial and error. Remember, there is no such thing as a zero delay. By definition, you have to wait at least one trading period before buying or selling, because the market will be closed by the time you receive the latest price to plot.

Generally, a signal delay of two days on daily charts and one week on weekly charts gives the best results.

Using three moving averages

The use of two moving averages to obtain golden and dead crosses has been discussed in an earlier chapter. The use of three averages can significantly increase trading profits.

It is a technique which is often misunderstood and rarely used. It also works better with the INDEXIA filters than with other average types. The purpose of the third moving average is to act as an agitator or confirmer, thus ensuring that during the delay period, the signal is still in force. Note that this is not the same as ensuring that the signal has not reversed. To explain this, let's look at the rules for a buy signal with a two-day delay.

A buy alert is given when the short-term moving average crosses above both the medium- and long-term averages. For the buy alert to be confirmed and converted into a buy signal, the short must remain above the medium and long for the period of the delay. So let's assume that the short goes above the medium and long to give a buy alert. Four things can happen:

1. The short stays above for one day, then crosses back through the medium, but not the long. This does not reverse the buy alert into a sell but simply puts the buy alert on hold, by not converting it into a buy signal. The buy alert therefore remains in force.
2. The short stays above for one day, but then crosses back through the medium, but not the long. As above, the buy alert is not reversed. If however, the short then continues down and crosses back through the long-term average as well, the buy alert is cancelled and the previous sell signal remains in force.
3. The short stays above for one day, but then crosses back through the medium, but not the long. Again, this puts the buy alert on hold. If the short then crosses above the medium again, it must remain so for the period of the delay (two days in this example) to confirm the buy. This crossing back and forth can go on for some time while there is uncertainty as to the signal.
4. The short stays above the medium and long for the two days of the delay. The buy alert becomes a buy signal which can then only be reversed into a sell signal by the short going below the medium and the long for two days.

Unfortunately, although the three average technique tends to produce superior results, it is more difficult to refine because it is necessary to decide not only on three moving average periods, but also on the delay which has the effect of changing the best moving average periods again.

Choosing moving average periods

The choice of the best periods to use for moving averages has plagued analysts for years. Recent moving average optimisation software has made the task a lot easier, but it is still a time-consuming task. For consistency and general reliability, however, it is hard to beat numbers from the Fibonacci time series. The series is as follows: 1, 1, 2, 3, 5, 8, 13, 21, 34, 55, 89, 144, 233, etc. For consistency, the 13, 21 and 34 average periods will be used throughout this chapter.

Moving averages and the Crash

It may be some time since the infamous Crash of 1987, but it has left an indelible imprint on the memory of many an investor. So much so, that the first question many people ask is, 'How did the indicator perform in October 1987'? Chart 6.6 shows the FTSE 100 index on a weekly basis before and after the Crash with each of the three moving average types drawn.

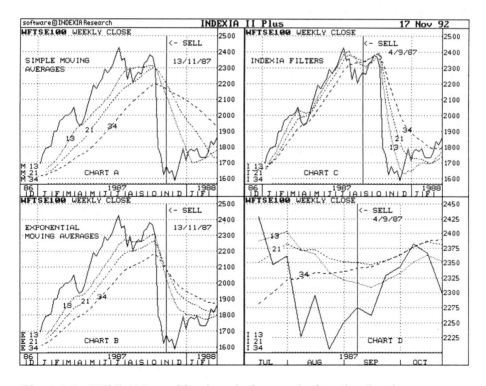

Chart 6.6   FTSE 100 weekly close before and after the Crash

The sell signal given by the three simple moving averages (top left) is disastrous. Using only a one week signal delay, it put you into the market on 28 November 1986, but gave a sell signal on 13 November 1987, virtually a month after the Crash had occurred, and almost at the bottom of the market. This reduced the gain from the year's run up to the Crash to a mere 2.5 per cent. The sell signal given by the exponential averages (bottom left) is just as unsatisfactory – also on 13 November, long after the Crash itself. The result produced by the INDEXIA filters is more encouraging. Having put you in on 16 January 1987, it took you out on 4 September 1987, a full month before the Crash. What is interesting is that even though the market rallied again into October (a rally that caught many an experienced trader), the filters remained in a downtrend thus avoiding a disastrous whipsaw at the top of the market. A close-up view is provided (bottom right) showing the performance of the INDEXIA filters during August, September and October 1987.

This example shows how these proprietary moving averages have revolutionised the way in which moving averages are regarded. As one would expect, the filters are not infallible: they can result in trading losses, but overall they produce far better results than either the simple or the exponential.

The FTSE 100 since 1984 on a weekly basis

Having looked at the 1987 Crash, let's examine the FTSE 100 Index since January 1984. Tables 6.1–6.3 show all the buy and sell signals for the FTSE

Table 6.1   Simple moving averages – FTSE trades since January 1984

Date open	Price open	Date close	Price close	Gain/loss on trade (%)
070984	1099.3	230885	1313.5	19.5
111085	1322.3	031086	1560.8	18.0
281186	1636.7	131187	1678.3	2.5
030688	1819.2	111188	1802.7	−0.9
100289	2056.1	291289	2422.7	17.8
020290	2355.1	120490	2222.1	−5.6
270790	2330.1	210990	2025.5	−13.1
010391	2386.9	201291	2358.1	−1.2
010592	2659.8	210892	2365.7	−11.1
Total				26.0

Table 6.2 Exponential moving averages – FTSE trades since January 1984

Date open	Price open	Date close	Price close	Gain/loss on trade (%)
240884	1087.2	131187	1678.3	54.4
120888	1843.4	090988	1738.4	−5.7
270189	2005.9	270490	2106.6	5.0
150690	2392.3	310890	2162.8	−9.6
010391	2386.9	271291	2418.7	1.3
280292	2562.1	030492	2382.7	−7.0
240492	2643.0	310792	2399.6	−9.2
301092	2658.3	131192	2697.5	1.5
Total				30.70

Table 6.3 Indexia filters – FTSE trades since January 1984

Date open	Price open	Date close	Price close	Gain/loss on trade (%)
170884	1074.9	070685	1310.6	21.9
081185	1390.1	130686	1582.4	13.8
160187	1789.0	040987	2274.9	27.2
060588	1801.1	230988	1792.4	−0.5
141088	1840.6	161288	1773.9	−3.6
200189	1917.5	201089	2179.1	13.6
120190	2380.1	020290	2355.1	−1.1
220690	2378.5	170890	2176.9	−8.5
281290	2160.4	181091	2601.1	20.4
010592	2659.8	100792	2490.8	−6.4
161092	2563.9	131192	2697.5	5.2
Total				82.2

100 on a weekly basis since 1984, as well as the percentage gain or loss on each trade using the 13, 21 and 34-day INDEXIA, simple and exponential.

Table 6.1 shows the buy and sell signals since January 1984 using the 13, 21 and 34-week simple moving averages and a one-week signal delay. Table 6.2 shows the buy and sell signals since January 1984 using the 13, 21 and 34-week exponential moving averages and a one-week signal delay. Table 6.3 shows the buy and sell signals since January 1984 using

Table 6.4 Summary of simple, exponential and INDEXIA results

Moving average type	Winning trades	Losing trades	Total trades	Best gain	Worst loss	Total gain/loss
Simple	4	5	9	19.5%	−13.1%	26.0%
Exponential	4	4	8	54.4%	−9.6%	30.9%
INDEXIA	6	5	11	27.2%	−8.5%	82.4%

the 13, 21 and 34-week INDEXIA filters and a one-week signal delay. In each case, dealing costs have been ignored. The results are summarized in Table 6.4.

The INDEXIA filters yielded a total profit of 82.4 per cent, which is more than double the gains achieved by the simple and the exponential. In addition, the worst trading loss was only −8.5 per cent, the lowest of the three. The exponential yielded the best trading gain of 54.4 per cent, which happened to be the first trade and which lasted over three years! However, if you look at the other exponential trades, the second and third best were only 5 and 1.5 per cent. The INDEXIA filters, on the other hand, yielded second and third best trades of 21.9 and 20.4 per cent. Although having two good trades of 19.5 and 18.0 per cent, the simple yielded the worst losing trade and consequently the lowest total percentage gain.

The FTSE 100 since 1984 on a daily basis

A similar exercise was conducted on the FTSE 100 on a daily basis since 1984. Once again the INDEXIA filters yielded a superior profit. The signal delay was extended to two days and the results are summarized in Table 6.5.

Table 6.5 Summary of trades on the daily FTSE

Moving average type	Winning trades	Losing trades	Total trades	Best gain	Worst loss	Total gain/loss
Simple	18	15	33	19.5%	−21.5%	51.7%
Exponential	12	15	27	24.8%	−16.7%	73.0%
INDEXIA	23	14	37	22.7%	−10.9%	130.7%

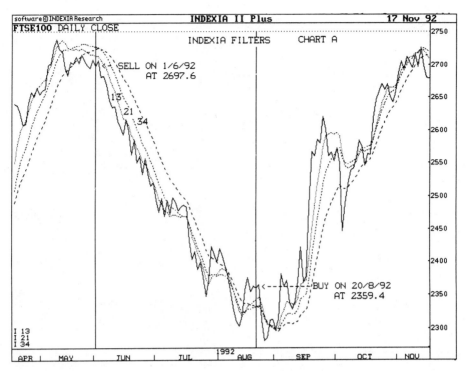

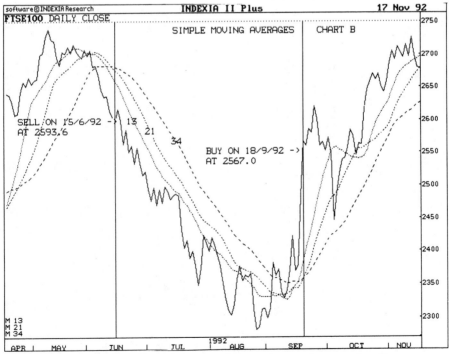

Chart 6.7 INDEXIA filters vs. simple moving averages, April–
November 1992

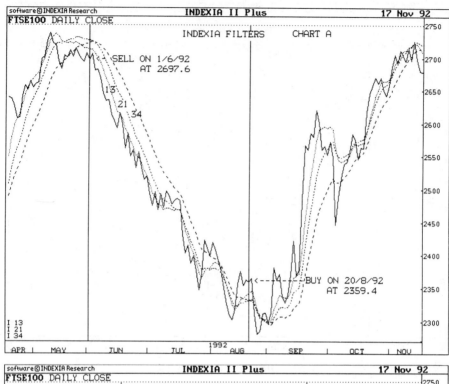

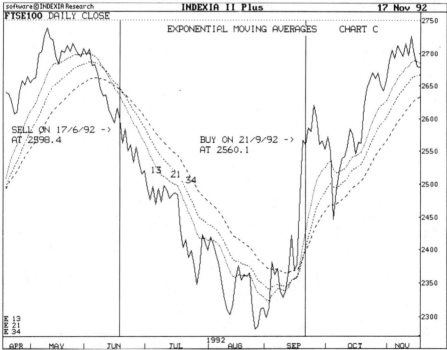

Chart 6.8 INDEXIA filters vs. exponential moving averages, April–November 1992

The gain on the INDEXIA filters of 130.7 per cent is almost double that achieved by the exponential averages.

Charts 6.7 and 6.8 provide a comparison of the timing of the last two signals by the three average types. In each case, the top chart (A) shows the signals given by the INDEXIA filters, while the bottom chart (B) shows simple moving averages and the bottom chart (C) shows exponential moving averages.

The INDEXIA filters gave a sell signal on 1 June at 2697.6, two days before the FTSE 100 index broke down. The simple and exponential on the other hand, gave sell signals two weeks later and 100 points lower on 15 and 17 June at 2593.6 and 2598.4 respectively.

The INDEXIA filter buy signal is also quite extraordinary. The signal came on 20 August, four days before the bottom – even after waiting the required two days! The simple and exponential average buy signals came a month later on 18 and 21 September, 200 points higher than the INDEXIA filter and almost at the same level as the previous sell signal.

As the FTSE 100 is an option instrument, the downside profit is just as important as the upside. The fact that you could have bought a put option on 1 June and sold it on 20 August for a 338 point move, make the INDEXIA filters worth considering as a trading tool.

Equity traded options

We have looked at how the various moving average types have performed on the FTSE 100 Index, now let's examine how they have performed with some of the equity traded option underlying securities. Before taking action in the traded options market, many traders monitor the performance of the underlying security first. Moving averages are an excellent way of obtaining objective buy and sell signals.

A true test of moving averages is the way in which they handle sideways movements or consolidations. The truth is that most moving averages suffer badly during these periods. However, INDEXIA filters work well during consolidation phases.

The following examination of 11 underlying securities (see Charts 6.9–6.19 and Tables 6.6–6.16), shows direct comparisons between simple, exponential and INDEXIA filters over a year of price movement. As the signals given by simple averages are so similar to those given by exponential averages, the charts only show the INDEXIA filters and simple moving averages, although the tables show all three types. As we are dealing with option stocks, both long and short trades have been considered.

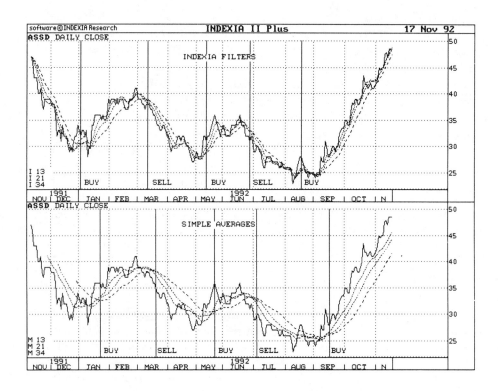

Chart 6.9   INDEXIA filters vs. simple averages for ASDA, November 1991–November 1992

Table 6.6   Trades in Asda by average type

INDEXIA filters

‹- - - - - - - - Long - - - - - - - -›				‹- - - - - - - - Short - - - - - - - -›			
‹- - open - -›		‹- - close - -›	%	‹- - open - -›		‹- - close - -›	%
030192	32.0	110392	38.0	18.8	110392	38.0	130592	31.0	22.6
130592	31.0	260692	31.0	0.0	260692	31.0	180892	28.0	10.7
180892	28.0	171192	48.5	73.2			Total	33.3
		Total	92.0				

Simple moving averages

‹- - - - - - - - Long - - - - - - - -›				‹- - - - - - - - Short - - - - - - - -›			
‹- - open - -›		‹- - close - -›	%	‹- - open - -›		‹- - close - -›	%
230192	36.0	190392	35.0	-2.8	281191	39.0	230192	36.0	8.3
210592	36.0	030792	30.0	-16.7	190392	35.0	210592	36.0	-2.8
160992	28.0	171192	48.5	73.2	030792	30.0	160992	28.0	7.1
		Total	53.8			Total	12.7

Exponential moving averages

‹- - - - - - - - Long - - - - - - - -›				‹- - - - - - - - Short - - - - - - - -›			
‹- - open - -›		‹- - close - -›	%	‹- - open - -›		‹- - close - -›	%
290192	35.0	200392	34.0	-2.9	200392	34.0	220592	35.0	-2.9
220592	35.0	010792	29.0	-17.1	010792	29.0	150992	28.0	3.6
150992	28.0	171192	48.5	73.2			Total	0.7
		Total	53.2				

- INDEXIA filters provided 3 long trades for a 92 per cent gain, of which 0 were losing.
- INDEXIA filters provided 2 short trades for a 33 per cent gain, of which 0 were losing.
- Simple averages provided 3 long trades, for a 53.8 per cent gain, of which 2 were losing.
- Simple averages provided 3 short trades, for a 12.7 per cent gain, of which 1 was losing.
- Exponential averages provided 3 long trades, for a 53.2 per cent gain, of which 2 were losing.
- Exponential averages provided 2 short trades, for a 0.7 per cent gain, of which 1 was losing.

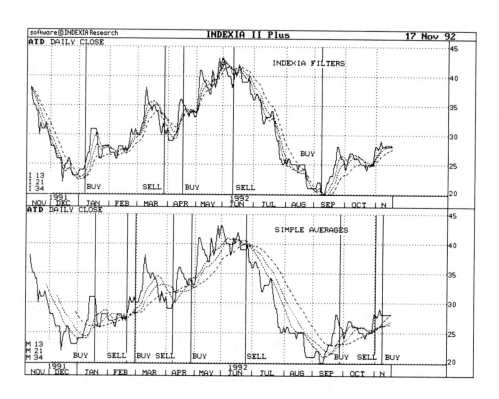

Chart 6.10   INDEXIA filters vs. simple averages for Amstrad,
November 1991–November 1992

Table 6.7   Trades in Amstrad by average type

INDEXIA filters

‹- - - - - - - - Long - - - - - - - -›					‹- - - - - - - - Short - - - - - - - -›				
‹- - open - -›		‹- - close - -›		%	‹- - open - -›		‹- - close - -›		%
080192	25.0	270392	31.0	24.0	270392	31.0	150492	35.0	−11.4
150492	35.0	100692	39.0	11.4	100692	39.0	080992	20.0	95.0
080992	20.0	171192	28.0	40.0					
		Total		75.4			Total		83.6

Simple moving averages

‹- - - - - - - - Long - - - - - - - -›					‹- - - - - - - - Short - - - - - - - -›				
‹- - open - -›		‹- - close - -›		%	‹- - open - -›		‹- - close - -›		%
200192	31.0	200292	28.0	−9.7	281191	30.0	200192	31.0	−3.2
280292	30.0	070492	30.0	0.0	200292	28.0	280292	30.0	−6.7
280492	34.0	240692	39.0	14.7	070492	30.0	280492	34.0	−11.8
280992	26.0	021192	28.0	7.7	240692	39.0	280992	26.0	50.0
091192	28.0	171192	28.0	0.0	021192	28.0	091192	28.0	0.0
		Total		12.7			Total		28.3

Exponential moving averages

‹- - - - - - - - Long - - - - - - - -›					‹- - - - - - - - Short - - - - - - - -›				
‹- - open - -›		‹- - close - -›		%	‹- - open - -›		‹- - close - -›		%
210192	29.0	110292	28.0	−3.4	110292	28.0	250292	30.0	−6.7
250292	30.0	060492	29.0	−3.3	060492	29.0	150492	35.0	−17.1
150492	35.0	020792	37.0	5.7	020792	37.0	290992	26.0	42.3
290992	26.0	171192	28.0	7.7					
		Total		6.6			Total		18.50

- INDEXIA filters provided 3 long trades for a 75.4 per cent gain, of which 0 were losing.
- INDEXIA filters provided 2 short trades for a 83.6 per cent gain, of which 1 was losing.
- Simple averages provided 5 long trades, for a 12.7 per cent gain, of which 1 was losing.
- Simple averages provided 5 short trades, for a 28.3 per cent gain, of which 3 were losing.
- Exponential averages provided 4 long trades, for a 6.6 per cent gain, of which 2 were losing.
- Exponential averages provided 3 short trades, for a 18.5 per cent gain, of which 2 were losing.

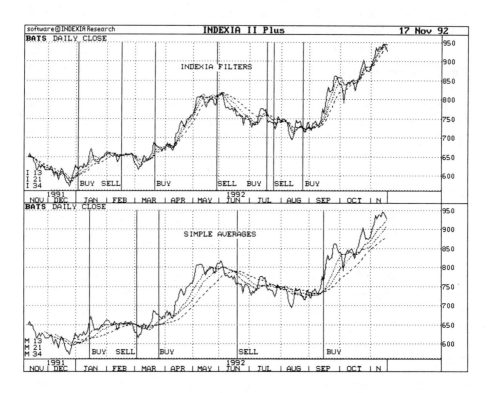

Chart 6.11   INDEXIA filters vs. simple averages for BAT Industries, November 1991–November 1992

Table 6.8 Trades in BAT Industries by average type

INDEXIA filters

‹- - - - - - - - Long - - - - - - - -›			‹- - - - - - - - Short - - - - - - - -›		
‹- - open - -›	‹- - close - -›	%	‹- - open - -›	‹- - close - -›	%
030192 615.0	170292 655.0	6.5	191191 614.0	030192 615.0	−0.2
200392 686.0	280592 807.0	17.6	170292 655.0	200392 686.0	−4.5
170792 750.0	240792 732.0	−2.4	280592 807.0	170792 750.0	7.6
240892 724.0	171192 928.0	28.2	240792 732.0	240892 724.0	1.1
	Total	49.9		Total	4.0

Simple moving averages

‹- - - - - - - - Long - - - - - - - -›			‹- - - - - - - - Short - - - - - - - -›		
‹- - open - -›	‹- - close - -›	%	‹- - open - -›	‹- - close - -›	%
150192 662.0	030392 627.0	−5.3	281191 615.0	150192 662.0	−7.1
250392 674.0	180692 758.0	12.5	030392 627.0	250392 674.0	−7.0
150992 764.0	171192 928.0	21.5	180692 758.0	150992 764.0	−0.8
	Total	28.6		Total	−14.9

Exponential moving averages

‹- - - - - - - - Long - - - - - - - -›			‹- - - - - - - - Short - - - - - - - -›		
‹- - open - -›	‹- - close - -›	%	‹- - open - -›	‹- - close - -›	%
140192 638.0	060392 625.0	−2.0	191191 614.0	140192 638.0	−3.8
190392 687.0	240692 733.0	6.7	060392 625.0	190392 687.0	−9.0
160992 788.0	171192 928.0	17.8	240692 733.0	160992 788.0	−7.0
	Total	22.4		Total	−19.8

- INDEXIA filters provided 4 long trades for a 49.9 per cent gain, of which 1 was losing.
- INDEXIA filters provided 4 short trades for a 4 per cent gain, of which 2 were losing.
- Simple averages provided 3 long trades, for a 28.6 per cent gain, of which 1 was losing.
- Simple averages provided 3 short trades, for a 14.9 per cent loss, of which all 3 were losing.
- Exponential averages provided 3 long trades, for a 22.4 per cent gain, of which 1 was losing.
- Exponential averages provided 3 short trades, for a 19.8 per cent loss, of which all 3 were losing.

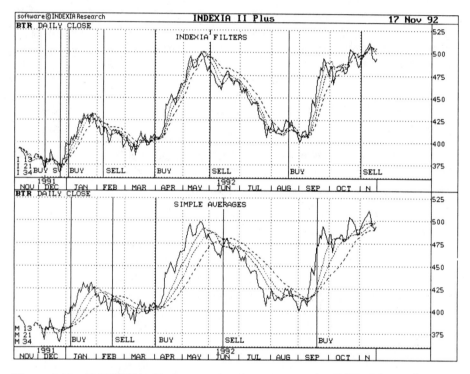

Chart 6.12   INDEXIA filters vs. simple averages for BTR, November
1991–November 1992

Table 6.9 Trades in BTR by average type

INDEXIA filters

‹- - - - - - - - Long - - - - - - - -›				‹- - - - - - - - Short - - - - - - - -›			
‹- - open - -›		‹- - close - -›	%	‹- - open - -›		‹- - close - -›	%
161291	381.0	231291 366.0	−3.9	151191	386.0	161291 381.0	1.3
030192	396.0	070292 409.0	3.3	231291	366.0	030192 396.0	−7.6
310392	409.0	010692 481.0	17.6	070292	409.0	310392 409.0	0.0
190892	424.0	021192 492.5	16.2	010692	481.0	190892 424.0	13.4
				021192	492.5	171192 494.0	−0.3
		Total	33.1			Total	6.9

Simple moving averages

‹- - - - - - - - Long - - - - - - - -›				‹- - - - - - - - Short - - - - - - - -›			
‹- - open - -›		‹- - close - -›	%	‹- - open - -›		‹- - close - -›	%
070192	406.0	180292 414.0	2.0	281191	387.0	070192 406.0	−4.7
010492	405.0	150692 473.0	16.8	180292	414.0	010492 405.0	2.2
180992	473.5	171192 494.0	4.3	150692	473.0	180992 473.5	−0.1
		Total	23.1			Total	−2.6

Exponential moving averages

‹- - - - - - - - Long - - - - - - - -›				‹- - - - - - - - Short - - - - - - - -›			
‹- - open - -›		‹- - close - -›	%	‹- - open - -›		‹- - close - -›	%
060192	397.0	020392 399.0	0.5	151191	386.0	060192 397.0	−2.8
030492	404.0	020792 455.0	12.6	020392	399.0	030492 404.0	−1.2
170992	460.0	171192 494.0	7.4	020792	455.0	170992 460.0	−1.1
		Total	20.5			Total	−5.1

- INDEXIA filters provided 4 long trades for a 33.1 per cent gain, of which 1 was losing.
- INDEXIA filters provided 5 short trades for a 6.9 per cent gain, of which 2 were losing.
- Simple averages provided 3 long trades, for a 23.1 per cent gain, of which 0 were losing.
- Simple averages provided 3 short trades, for a 2.6 per cent loss, of which 2 were losing.
- Exponential averages provided 3 long trades, for a 20.5 per cent gain, of which 0 were losing.
- Exponential averages provided 3 short trades, for a 5.1 per cent loss, of which all 3 were losing.

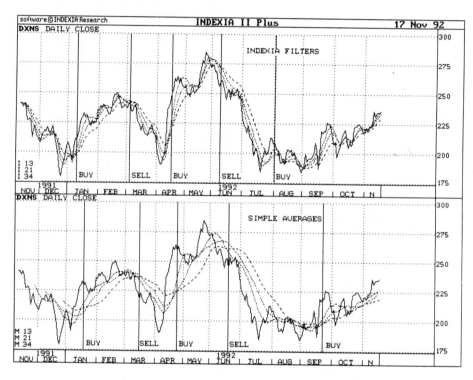

Chart 6.13 INDEXIA filters vs. simple averages for Dixons, November 1991–November 1992

Table 6.10 Trades in Dixons by average type

INDEXIA filters

‹- - - - - - - - Long - - - - - - - -›				‹- - - - - - - - Short - - - - - - - -›			
‹- - open - -›	‹- - close - -›		%	‹- - open - -›	‹- - close - -›		%
100192	211.0	040392 241.0	14.2	131191	238.0	100192 211.0	12.8
150492	250.0	090692 260.0	4.0	040392	241.0	150492 250.0	−3.6
030892	209.0	171192 236.0	12.9	090692	260.0	030892 209.0	24.4
		Total	31.1			Total	33.6

Simple moving averages

‹- - - - - - - - Long - - - - - - - -›				‹- - - - - - - - Short - - - - - - - -›			
‹- - open - -›	‹- - close - -›		%	‹- - open- -›	‹- - close - -›		%
200192	229.0	160392 218.0	−4.8	281191	212.0	200192 229.0	−7.4
240492	259.0	180692 245.0	−5.4	160392	218.0	240492 259.0	−15.8
220992	219.0	171192 236.0	7.8	180692	245.0	220992 219.0	11.9
		Total	−2.4			Total	−11.4

Exponential moving averages

‹- - - - - - - - Long - - - - - - - -›				‹- - - - - - - - Short - - - - - - - -›			
‹- - open - -›	‹- - close - -›		%	‹- - open - -›	‹- - close - -›		%
200192	229.0	180392 219.0	−4.4	131191	238.0	200192 229.0	3.9
210492	262.0	220692 248.0	−5.3	180392	219.0	210492 262.0	−16.4
230992	219.0	171192 236.0	7.8	220692	248.0	230992 219.0	13.2
		Total	−1.9			Total	0.8

- INDEXIA filters provided 3 long trades for a 31.1 per cent gain, of which 0 were losing.
- INDEXIA filters provided 3 short trades for a 33.6 per cent gain, of which 1 was losing.
- Simple averages provided 3 long trades, for a 2.4 per cent loss, of which 2 were losing.
- Simple averages provided 3 short trades, for a 11.4 per cent loss, of which 2 were losing.
- Exponential averages provided 3 long trades, for a 1.9 per cent loss, of which 2 were losing.
- Exponential averages provided 3 short trades, for a 0.8 per cent gain, of which 1 was losing.

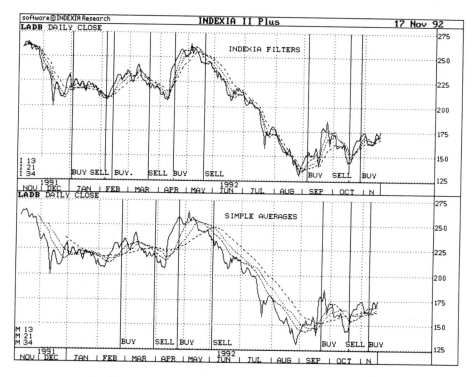

Chart 6.14   INDEXIA filters vs. simple averages for Ladbrokes, November 1991–November 1992

Table 6.11   Trades in Ladbrokes by average type

INDEXIA filters

‹- - - - - - - - Long - - - - - - - -›				‹- - - - - - - - Short - - - - - - - -›			
‹- - open - -›		‹- - close - -›	%	‹- - open - -›		‹- - close - -›	%
030192	219.0	060292 208.0	−5.0	251191	257.0	030192 219.0	17.4
130292	221.0	200392 217.0	−1.8	060292	208.0	130292 221.0	−5.9
150492	244.0	200592 243.0	−0.4	200392	217.0	150492 244.0	−11.1
040992	150.0	161092 144.0	−4.0	200592	243.0	040992 150.0	62.0
281092	172.0	171192 175.0	1.7	161092	144.0	281092 172.0	−16.3
		Total	−9.5			Total	46.1

Simple moving averages

‹- - - - - - - - Long - - - - - - - -›				‹- - - - - - - - Short - - - - - - - -›			
‹- - open - -›		‹- - close - -›	%	‹- - open - -›		‹- - close - -›	%
250292	232.0	300392 219.0	−5.6	281191	245.0	250292 232.0	5.6
240492	258.0	020692 236.0	−8.5	300392	219.0	240492 258.0	−15.1
220992	176.0	201092 149.0	−15.3	020692	236.0	220992 176.0	34.1
091192	162.0	171192 175.0	8.0	201092	149.0	091192 162.0	−8.0
		Total	−21.4			Total	16.6

Exponential moving averages

‹- - - - - - - - Long - - - - - - - -›				‹- - - - - - - - Short - - - - - - - -›			
‹- - open - -›		‹- - close - -›	%	‹- - open - -›		‹- - close - -›	%
210292	225.0	240392 222.0	−1.3	261191	257.0	210292 225.0	14.2
160492	248.0	040692 234.0	−5.6	240392	222.0	160492 248.0	−10.5
240992	186.0	151092 143.0	−23.1	040692	234.0	240992 186.0	25.8
301092	174.0	171192 175.0	0.6	151092	143.0	301092 174.0	−17.8
		Total	−29.5			Total	11.70

- INDEXIA filters provided 5 long trades for a 9.5 per cent loss, of which 4 were losing.
- INDEXIA filters provided 5 short trades for a 46.1 per cent gain, of which 3 were losing.
- Simple averages provided 4 long trades, for a 21.4 per cent loss, of which 3 were losing.
- Simple averages provided 4 short trades, for a 16.6 per cent gain, of which 2 were losing.
- Exponential averages provided 4 long trades, for a 29.5 per cent loss, of which 3 were losing.
- Exponential averages provided 4 short trades, for a 11.7 per cent gain, of which 2 were losing.

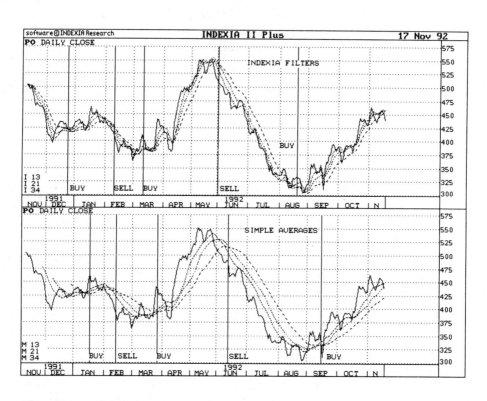

Chart 6.15   INDEXIA filters vs. simple averages for P & O, November
1991–November 1992

Table 6.12 Trades in P & O by average type

INDEXIA filters

‹-------- Long --------›					‹-------- Short --------›				
‹- - open - -›		‹- - close - -›		%	‹- - open - -›		‹- - close - -›		%
231291	420.0	110292	410.0	−2.4	110292	410.0	110392	402.0	2.0
110392	402.0	010692	508.0	26.4	010692	508.0	190892	333.0	52.6
190892	333.0	171192	440.0	32.1					
			Total	56.1				Total	54.5

Simple moving averages

‹-------- Long --------›					‹-------- Short --------›				
‹- - open - -›		‹- - close - -›		%	‹- - open - -›		‹- - close - -›		%
170192	463.0	130292	391.0	−15.6	281191	451.0	170192	463.0	−2.6
260392	439.0	110692	488.0	11.2	130292	391.0	260392	439.0	−10.9
150992	338.0	171192	440.0	30.2	110692	488.0	150992	338.0	44.4
			Total	25.8				Total	30.9

Exponential moving averages

‹-------- Long --------›					‹-------- Short --------›				
‹- - open - -›		‹- - close - -›		%	‹- - open - -›		‹- - close - -›		%
240192	447.0	060292	427.0	−4.5	060292	427.0	300392	429.0	−0.5
300392	429.0	160692	465.0	8.4	160692	465.0	240992	392.0	18.6
240992	392.0	171192	440.0	12.2					
			Total	16.2				Total	18.20

- INDEXIA filters provided 3 long trades for a 56.1 per cent gain, of which 1 was losing.
- INDEXIA filters provided 2 short trades for a 54.5 per cent gain, of which 0 were losing.
- Simple averages provided 3 long trades, for a 25.8 per cent gain, of which 1 was losing.
- Simple averages provided 3 short trades, for a 30.9 per cent gain, of which 2 were losing.
- Exponential averages provided 3 long trades, for a 16.2 per cent gain, of which 1 was losing.
- Exponential averages provided 2 short trades, for a 18.2 per cent gain, of which 1 was losing.

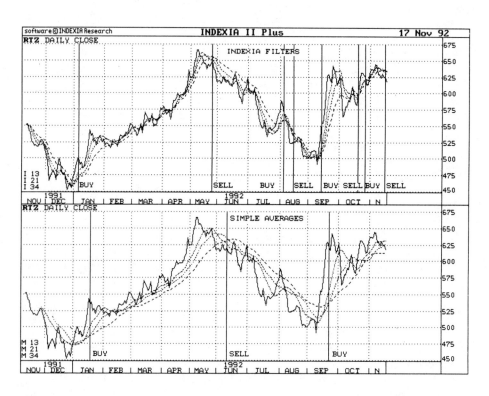

Chart 6.16 INDEXIA filters vs. simple averages for RTZ, November 1991–November 1992

Table 6.13   Trades in RTZ by average type

INDEXIA filters

‹- - - - - - - - Long - - - - - - - - -›				%	‹- - - - - - - - Short - - - - - - - - -›				%
‹- - open - -›		‹- - close - -›			‹- - open - -›		‹- - close - -›		
070192	500.0	260592	649.0	29.8	151191	526.0	070192	500.0	5.2
050892	568.0	140892	525.0	−7.6	260592	649.0	050892	568.0	14.3
140992	555.0	201092	602.0	8.5	140892	525.0	140992	555.0	−5.4
271092	624.0	161192	624.0	0.0	201092	602.0	271092	624.0	−3.5
					161192	624.0	171192	618.0	1.0
		Total		30.7			Total		11.5

Simple moving averages

‹- - - - - - - - Long - - - - - - - - -›				%	‹- - - - - - - - Short - - - - - - - - -›				%
‹- - open - -›		‹- - close - -›			‹- - open - -›		‹- - close - -›		
200192	534.0	100692	620.0	16.1	281191	520.0	200192	534.0	−2.6
220992	620.0	171192	618.0	−0.3	100692	620.0	220992	620.0	0.0
		Total		15.8			Total		−2.6

Exponential moving averages

‹- - - - - - - - Long - - - - - - - - -›				%	‹- - - - - - - - Short - - - - - - - - -›				%
‹- - open - -›		‹- - close - -›			‹- - open - -›		‹- - close - -›		
210192	538.0	230692	594.0	10.4	151191	526.0	210192	538.0	−2.2
210992	629.0	171192	618.0	−1.7	230692	594.0	210992	629.0	−5.6
		Total		8.7			Total		−7.8

- INDEXIA filters provided 4 long trades for a 30.7 per cent gain, of which 1 was losing.
- INDEXIA filters provided 5 short trades for a 11.5 per cent gain, of which 2 were losing.
- Simple averages provided 2 long trades, for a 15.8 per cent gain, of which 1 was losing.
- Simple averages provided 2 short trades, for a 2.6 per cent loss, of which 1 was losing.
- Exponential averages provided 2 long trades, for a 8.7 per cent gain, of which 1 was losing.
- Exponential averages provided 2 short trades, for a 7.8 per cent loss, of which 2 were losing.

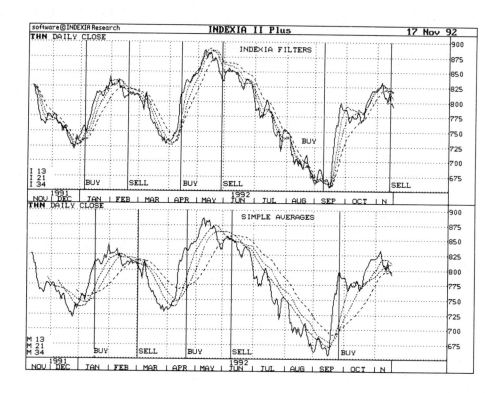

Chart 6.17   INDEXIA filters vs. simple averages for Thorn EMI, November 1991–November 1992

Table 6.14 Trades in Thorn EMI by average type

INDEXIA filters

‹- - - - - - - - Long - - - - - - - - -›					‹- - - - - - - - Short - - - - - - - - -›				
‹- - open - -›		‹- - close - -›		%	‹- - open - -›		‹- - close - -›		%
070192	756.0	190292	813.0	7.5	131191	810.0	070192	756.0	7.1
130492	815.0	280592	835.0	2.5	190292	813.0	130492	815.0	−0.2
090992	670.0	131192	800.0	19.4	280592	835.0	090992	670.0	24.6
					131192	800.0	171192	792.0	1.0
			Total	29.4				Total	32.5

Simple moving averages

‹- - - - - - - - Long - - - - - - - - -›					‹- - - - - - - - Short - - - - - - - - -›				
‹- - open - -›		‹- - close - -›		%	‹- - open - -›		‹- - close - -›		%
170192	815.0	020392	807.0	−1.0	281191	777.0	170192	815.0	−4.7
220492	832.0	090692	852.0	2.4	020392	807.0	220492	832.0	−3.0
250992	799.0	171192	792.0	−0.9	090692	852.0	250992	799.0	6.6
			Total	0.5				Total	−1.0

Exponential moving averages

‹- - - - - - - - Long - - - - - - - - -›					‹- - - - - - - - Short - - - - - - - - -›				
‹- - open - -›		‹- - close - -›		%	‹- - open - -›		‹- - close - -›		%
170192	815.0	120392	770.0	−5.5	131191	810.0	170192	815.0	−0.6
160492	835.0	190692	830.0	−0.6	120392	770.0	160492	835.0	−7.8
250992	799.0	171192	792.0	−0.9	190692	830.0	250992	799.0	3.9
			Total	−7.0				Total	−4.5

- INDEXIA filters provided 3 long trades for a 29.4 per cent gain, of which 0 were losing.
- INDEXIA filters provided 4 short trades for a 32.5 per cent gain, of which 1 was losing.
- Simple averages provided 3 long trades, for a 0.5 per cent gain, of which 2 were losing.
- Simple averages provided 3 short trades, for a 1.0 per cent loss, of which 2 were losing.
- Exponential averages provided 3 long trades, for a 7.0 per cent loss, of which all 3 were losing.
- Exponential averages provided 3 short trades, for a 4.5 per cent loss, of which 2 were losing.

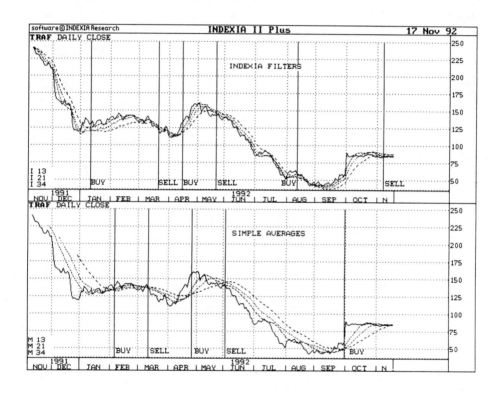

Chart 6.18   INDEXIA filters vs. simple averages for Trafalgar House, November 1991–November 1992

Table 6.15 Trades in Trafalgar House by average type

INDEXIA filters

‹- - - - - - - - Long - - - - - - - - -›					‹- - - - - - - - Short - - - - - - - - -›				
‹- - open - -›		‹- - close - -›		%	‹- - open - -›		‹- - close - -›		%
130192	130.0	200392	119.0	−8.5	200392	119.0	140492	133.0	−10.5
140492	133.0	210592	142.0	6.8	210592	142.0	120892	58.0	144.8
120892	58.0	061192	83.5	44.0	061192	83.5	171192	84.5	−1.2
		Total		42.3			Total		133.1

Simple moving averages

‹- - - - - - - - Long - - - - - - - - -›					‹- - - - - - - - Short - - - - - - - - -›				
‹- - open - -›		‹- - close - -›		%	‹- - open - -›		‹- - close - -›		%
060292	138.0	110392	136.0	−1.4	281191	210.0	060292	138.0	52.2
270492	156.0	020692	140.0	−10.3	110392	136.0	270492	156.0	−12.8
300992	60.5	171192	84.5	39.7	020692	140.0	300992	60.5	131.4
		Total		28.0			Total		170.8

Exponential moving averages

‹- - - - - - - - Long - - - - - - - - -›					‹- - - - - - - - Short - - - - - - - - -›				
‹- - open - -›		‹- - close - -›		%	‹- - open - -›		‹- - close - -›		%
230492	147.0	050692	136.0	−7.5	050692	136.0	051092	84.0	61.9
051092	84.0	171192	84.5	0.6					
		Total		−6.9			Total		61.9

- INDEXIA filters provided 3 long trades for a 42.3 per cent gain, of which 1 was losing.
- INDEXIA filters provided 3 short trades for a 133.1 per cent gain, of which 2 were losing.
- Simple averages provided 3 long trades, for a 28.0 per cent gain, of which 2 were losing.
- Simple averages provided 3 short trades, for a 170.8 per cent gain, of which 1 was losing.
- Exponential averages provided 2 long trades, for a 6.9 per cent loss, of which 1 was losing.
- Exponential averages provided only 1 short trade, for a 61.9 per cent gain.

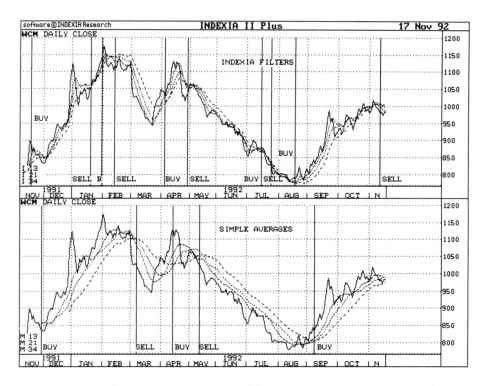

Chart 6.19 INDEXIA filters vs. simple averages for Wellcome,
November1991–November 1992

Table 6.16   Trades in Wellcome by average type

INDEXIA filters

‹- - - - - - - - Long - - - - - - - -›				‹- - - - - - - - Short - - - - - - - -›			
‹- - open - -›	‹- - close - -›		%	‹- - open - -›	‹- - close - -›		%
181191	893.0	210192 1055.0	18.1	210192	1055.0	310192 1147.0	−8.0
310192	1147.0	130292 1117.0	−2.6	130292	1117.0	030492 1028.0	8.7
030492	1028.0	290492 1036.0	0.8	290492	1036.0	150792 878.0	18.0
150792	878.0	240792 826.0	−5.9	240792	826.0	180892 788.0	4.8
180892	788.0	111192 978.0	24.1	111192	978.0	171192 982.0	−0.4
		Total	34.5			Total	23.0

Simple moving averages

‹- - - - - - - - Long - - - - - - - -›				‹- - - - - - - - Short - - - - - - - -›			
‹- - open - -›	‹- - close - -›		%	‹- - open - -›	‹- - close - -›		%
281191	836.0	060392 1023.0	22.4	060392	1023.0	130492 1131.0	−9.5
130492	1131.0	130592 1028.0	−9.1	130592	1028.0	080992 834.0	23.3
080992	834.0	171192 982.0	17.7				
		Total	31.0			Total	13.7

Exponential moving averages

‹- - - - - - - - Long - - - - - - - -›				‹- - - - - - - - Short - - - - - - - -›			
‹- - open - -›	‹- - close - -›		%	‹- - open - -›	‹- - close - -›		%
181191	893.0	090392 1013.0	13.4	090392	1013.0	100492 1121.0	−9.6
100492	1121.0	140592 1016.0	−9.4	140592	1016.0	140992 884.0	14.9
140992	884.0	171192 982.0	11.1				
		Total	15.2			Total	5.3

- INDEXIA filters provided 5 long trades for a 34.5 per cent gain, of which 2 were losing.
- INDEXIA filters provided 5 short trades for a 23.0 per cent gain, of which 2 were losing.
- Simple averages provided 3 long trades, for a 31.0 per cent gain, of which 1 was losing.
- Simple averages provided 2 short trades, for a 13.7 per cent gain, of which 1 was losing.
- Exponential averages provided 3 long trades, for a 15.2 per cent gain, of which 1 was losing.
- Exponential averages provided 2 short trades, for a 5.3 per cent gain, of which 1 was losing.

Summary

A cursory glance over the preceding charts and tables shows the INDEXIA filters outperforming the other two averages in most respects, but let's try to summarize the results in tabular form. Table 6.17 shows the

Table 6.17 Summarized results on both long and short trades

Share	INDEXIA	Simple	Exponential
Asda	125.3%	66.5%	53.9%
Amstrad	159.0%	41.0%	25.1%
BAT	53.9%	13.7%	2.6%
BTR	40.0%	20.5%	15.4%
Dixons	64.7%	−13.8%	−1.1%
Ladbroke	36.6%	−4.8%	−17.8%
P & O	110.6%	56.7%	34.4%
RTZ	42.2%	13.2%	0.9%
Thorn EMI	61.9%	−0.5%	−11.5%
Trafalgar	175.4%	198.8%	55.0%
Wellcome	57.5%	44.7%	20.5%

total gain or loss from trading each share, taking advantage of long and short positions. In other words, a short is established at the same time as the long is closed and vice versa. The percentages in the table are obtained by a simple arithmetic sum of the total percentage gain on the longs and the shorts. While not being strictly correct, it is sufficient for comparison purposes, which is all we are interested in here.

Table 6.18 Summarized results of long trades

Average type	Total no. of long trades	No. of winning long trades	No. of losing long trades	Winning trades as a % of total	Sum of % gains/ losses
INDEXIA	40	29	11	72.5%	465.0%
Simple	35	21	14	60.0%	195.5%
Exponential	33	16	17	48.5%	97.5%

Table 6.18 concentrates on long trades only. In order to assess the reliability of the signals produced the table shows the number of winning and losing trades. It also expresses the number of winning trades as a percentage of the total. Once again, a simple sum of the percentage gains for each average type is inserted for comparison.

The INDEXIA filters yield more trades, but have fewer losing trades both in percentage and absolute terms.

Finally, Table 6.19 shows the same results as the previous table, but for the short trades.

Table 6.19 Summarized results of short trades

Average type	Total no. of short trades	No. of winning short trades	No. of losing short trades	Winning trades as a % of total	Sum of % gains/ losses
INDEXIA	40	24	16	60.0%	461.8%
Simple	33	13	20	39.4%	240.5%
Exponential	28	9	19	32.1%	79.9%

Once again, the INDEXIA filters yield far better results.

THE MACD INDICATOR AND INDEXIA FILTERS

The moving average convergence/divergence (MACD) indicator measures the difference between two moving averages. Traditionally it is based on the exponential moving average calculation. INDEXIA II Plus, however, allows the MACD to be based on the simple calculation as well as the INDEXIA filters. The results are very interesting.

The MACD simply charts the difference between two moving averages. Chart 6.20 shows the FTSE 100 Index with the three MACD types superimposed on one another below. Once again we have used two Fibonacci numbers for the moving average period. The MACD lines are marked for easy identification: MACD M is calculated with simple averages; MACD E is calculated with exponential averages (traditional method); and MACD I is calculated with INDEXIA filters. Notice the MACD I always turns first, then the MACD M and lastly the MACD E. This ties up with the results we obtained using the moving averages on the close price.

When the MACD crosses the zero line, it indicates that the two averages (34 and 21 in our example) which make up the MACD have

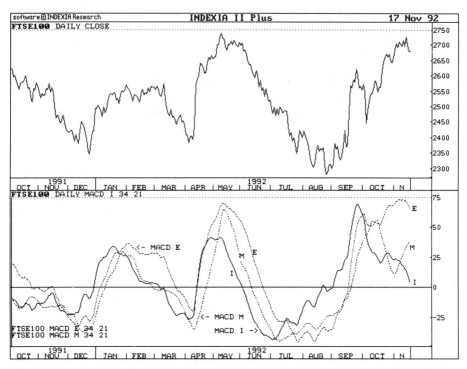

Chart 6.20   FTSE daily close and different MACD indicators, October 1991–November 1992

crossed. The MACD chart shows the exact point at which moving average crossovers occur. Notice the timing of the crossovers for the three different types of average. The INDEXIA filters are the leaders in each case.

MOVING AVERAGES ON THEIR OWN

We have so far looked at superimposing the various moving average types on to a closing price chart and comparing crossovers. Even the MACD measures the difference between two moving averages of the close price. We have also seen how closely the INDEXIA filter follows the price so that with shorter periods there is little or no lag effect. This makes the INDEXIA filter an ideal substitute for the price itself. The reason for wanting to do this is to eliminate whipsaws.

Chart 6.21 shows the FTSE 100 index with a 34-day INDEXIA filter. The problem with using one moving average like this is that it does produce a number of false signals. In an attempt to eliminate some of these, the lower chart shows first a 13-day INDEXIA filter standing-in for the close price chart. Then, a 34-day INDEXIA filter is calculated on the 13-day INDEXIA filter's figures and is superimposed. It is important to note that, in the lower chart, the 34-day INDEXIA filter is not calculated on the close price figures, but on the figures for the 13-day INDEXIA filter. Although the shape of the two 34 INDEXIA filters is similar, closer inspection reveals the lower 34-day filter is smoother, producing some excellent signals.

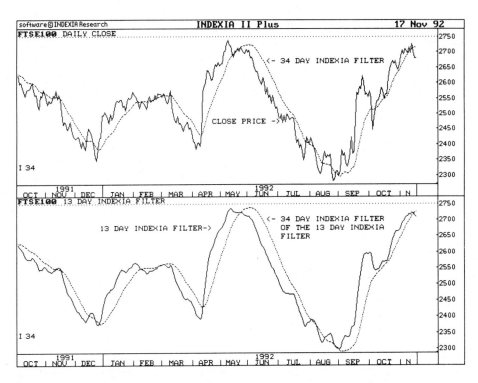

Chart 6.21   FTSE daily close and INDEXIA filters, October 1991–November 1992

CREATING INDICATORS BASED ON INDEXIA FILTERS

The INDEXIA II Plus study facility gives the analyst the ability to 'play around' with the charts in the system to create unique indicators with some very interesting results. Once again, we will look at how INDEXIA filters can be used to create a derivative of the well-known RSI oscillator.

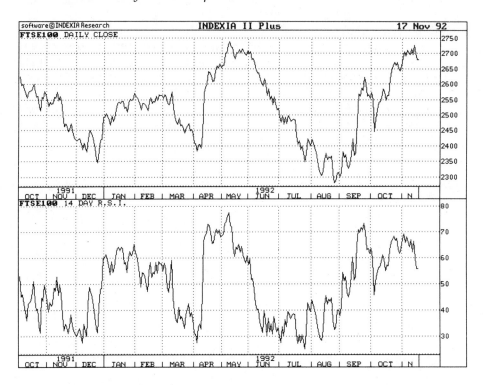

Chart 6.22   FTSE daily close and 14-day RSI, October 1991–November 1992

Chart 6.62 shows the FTSE 100 index with a traditional 14-day RSI drawn below. The RSI is an excellent timing tool, but it can be a difficult indicator to interpret on occasions.

Chart 6.23 shows, in the top window, a 13-day INDEXIA filter, which is once again standing in for the close price. The chart in the lower window is therefore a 14-day RSI, not of the close price, but of the 13-day INDEXIA filter. Look at how it has transformed the indicator. Without subjecting it to any significant lag, it has created a smooth oscillator which is far easier to read and interpret, but which still has the range. In fact it tends to oscillate closer to the zero and 100 extremes than the original RSI. This same technique can be applied to any oscillator, or even an on-balance volume chart.

CONCLUSION

This chapter has looked briefly at the INDEXIA II Plus system. The program has many unique tools and charts which have not been covered

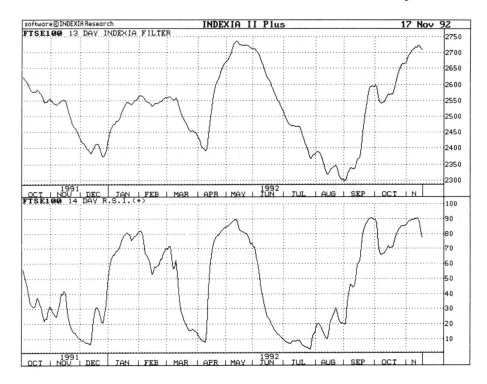

Chart 6.23   FTSE INDEXIA filter and 14-day RSI, October 1991–
November 1992

because of space limitations. We have shown that it is possible to obtain
reliable, objective trading signals using moving averages. What is
indisputable is that moving averages must play an important part in any
technical analyst's arsenal of techniques. We have also shown that
moving averages can be used to derive other indicators which are easier to
read and which can give less ambiguous results. In summary:

1. All average types incur losses as well as profits, although the
    INDEXIA filter losses appear to be less severe.
2. Buy and sell signals issued by the simple and exponential averages
    are often up to three weeks later than those issued by the INDEXIA
    filters.
3. Exponential averages, which are often held up as being superior
    because of their weighting factor, produce worse results than
    unweighted simple averages.
4. During sharp reversals of a trend, all average types failed to give
    timeous signals, including the INDEXIA filters, although they
    recovered far quicker than the other two. Moving average oscillators
    can assist during these times.

5. The INDEXIA filters often issue sell signals before the top and buy signals before the bottom.

6. All the tests were carried out using a standard set of moving averages, (13, 21 and 34). The results can therefore be improved by optimizing moving average periods. Moving average periods are dependent on the volatility of the particular share and so different periods work better for different shares. Research has also shown that it is possible to use a different set of averages for trading longs and shorts, the reason being that the market tends to exhibit a different pattern in downtrends.

Further information on the INDEXIA II Plus technical analysis system can be obtained from INDEXIA Research Ltd., PO Box 545, Berkhamsted, Herts HP4 3YJ, United Kingdom – telephone (0442) 878015, facsimile (0442) 876834.

7

Gann Analysis

William D. Gann (1878–1955) was a well-known stock and commodity trader at the beginning of this century. He developed his own trading techniques around mathematical formulae and geometrical patterns. There are a number of books devoted to the principles of Gann trading and I will not attempt to unfold the secrets of all his trading techniques in one chapter. Suffice to say, his techniques were very complicated. His basic premise revolved around cardinal squares, (the squaring of price and time), important highs and lows and retracements levels which, in turn, highlighted important areas of support and resistance. The geometrical patterns he mainly concentrated on were the 360 degree circle and its divisions.

THE CARDINAL SQUARE

This is a method used by Gann to determine future areas of support and resistance. An important low point is taken and placed in the centre of the square and then each higher price increment is entered in a clockwise direction. The numbers that fall in the cardinal cross portion of the square are then considered to be the most important levels of support and/or resistance.

For example, the low point of 2260 on the FTSE 100 towards the end of August (see Chart 7.1) can form the basis for two cardinal squares. The first cardinal square (see Table 7.1) is a matrix of size 13 with increments of 5 points and the second (Table 7.2) is a matrix of 13 with increments of 10 points (the choice depends on how sensitive you wish the areas of support and resistance to be and historically how successful they have been in the past).

Table 7.1 with increments of 5 points highlights support at 2455 and resistance at 2685. If we now turn back to Chart 7.1 for the FTSE 100 we can see that after the market rallied initially to 2660 in the middle of September, it fell back to this support level at just below 2455 (at the beginning of October) and then commenced a new rally to find resistance

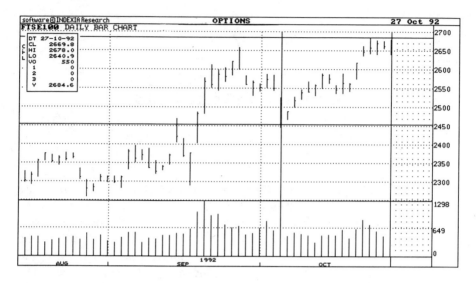

Chart 7.1   FTSE 100 daily bar chart, August–October 1992

Table 7.1   Gann cardinal square (matrix size 13; start value 2260; increment 5)

2920	2925	2930	2935	2940	2945	2950	2955	2960	2965	2970	2975	2980
2915	2710	2715	2720	2725	2730	2735	2740	2745	2750	2755	2760	2985
2910	2705	2540	2545	2550	2555	2560	2565	2570	2575	2580	2765	2990
2905	2700	2535	2410	2415	2420	2425	2430	2435	2440	2585	2770	2995
2900	2695	2530	2405	2320	2325	2330	2335	2340	2445	2590	2775	3000
2895	2690	2525	2400	2315	2270	2275	2280	2345	2450	2595	2780	3005
2890	2685	2520	2395	2310	2265	2260	2285	2350	2455	2600	2785	3010
2885	2680	2515	2390	2305	2300	2295	2290	2355	2460	2605	2790	3015
2880	2675	2510	2385	2380	2375	2370	2365	2360	2465	2610	2795	3020
2875	2670	2505	2500	2495	2490	2485	2480	2475	2470	2615	2800	3025
2870	2665	2660	2655	2650	2645	2640	2635	2630	2625	2620	2805	3030
2865	2860	2855	2850	2845	2840	2835	2830	2825	2820	2815	2810	3035
3100	3095	3090	3085	3080	3075	3070	3065	3060	3055	3050	3045	3040

again at the 2675 level (in the middle of October) as per the Gann cardinal square. The next resistance level was 2785 with possible intermediate support on a set back coming in at 2600. As mentioned earlier, these are

Table 7.2 Gann cardinal square (matrix size 13; start value 2260; increment 10)

3580	3590	3600	3610	3620	3630	3640	3650	3660	3670	3680	3690	3700
3570	3160	3170	3180	3190	3200	3210	3220	3230	3240	3250	3260	3710
3560	3150	2820	2830	2840	2850	2860	2870	2880	2890	2900	3270	3720
3550	3140	2810	2560	2570	2580	2590	2600	2610	2620	2910	3280	3730
3540	3130	2800	2550	2380	2390	2400	2410	2420	2630	2920	3290	3740
3530	3120	2790	2540	2370	2280	2290	2300	2430	2640	2930	3300	3750
3520	3110	2780	2530	2360	2270	2260	2310	2440	2650	2940	3310	3760
3510	3100	2770	2520	2350	2340	2330	2320	2450	2660	2950	3320	3770
3500	3090	2760	2510	2500	2490	2480	2470	2460	2670	2960	3330	3780
3490	3080	2750	2740	2730	2720	2710	2700	2690	2680	2970	3340	3790
3480	3070	3060	3050	3040	3030	3020	3010	3000	2990	2980	3350	3800
3470	3460	3450	3440	3430	3420	3410	3400	3390	3380	3370	3360	3810
3940	3930	3920	3910	3900	3890	3880	3870	3860	3850	3840	3830	3820

only guides to areas of support and resistance and can be used in conjuction with secondary indicators such as OB/OS, RSI, stochastics and the Fibonacci fans.

THE 360 DEGREE CIRCLE

This, together with its divisions, was Gann's favourite geometric pattern. Gann used these patterns to highlight natural areas of resistance used in determining tops and bottoms. The lower the division the stronger the level:

- full circles are the strongest – ie 360, 720, 1080, etc, indicated by 5 stars *****
- half circles are next – ie 180, 540, etc, indicated by 4 stars ****
- one-third circles are next – ie 120, 240, etc, indicated by 3 stars ***
- one-quarter circles are next – ie 90, 270, etc, indicated by 2 stars **
- one-eighth circles are next – ie 45, 135, etc, indicated by 1 star *
- one-sixteenth circles are next – ie 22.5, 67.5, etc, indicated by no stars.

The other divisions are the one-fifth circle and the one-sixth circle. The more important levels and their degree of importance in the first five circles are shown in Table 7.3.

Gann also used the divisions of the full circle to determine future

Table 7.3   Gann's 360 degree circle analysis

45*	405*	765*	1125*	1485*
60	420	780	1140	1500
72	432	752	1152	1512
90**	450**	810**	1170**	1530**
120***	480***	840***	1200***	1560***
144special	504	864	1224	1584
180****	540****	900****	1260****	1620****
216	576	936	1296	1656
225*	585*	945*	1305*	1665*
240***	600***	960***	1320***	1680***
270**	630**	990**	1350**	1710**
288	648	1008	1368	1728
300	660	1020	1380	1740
315*	675*	1035*	1395*	1755*
360*****	720*****	1080*****	1440*****	1800*****

Full circles for use over 2000 to 9000

6 circles	= 2160	17 circles	= 6120
7 circles	= 2520	18 circles	= 6480
8 circles	= 2880	19 circles	= 6840
9 circles	= 3240	20 circles	= 7200
10 circles	= 3600	21 circles	= 7560
11 circles	= 3960	22 circles	= 7920
13 circles	= 4680	23 circles	= 8280
14 circles	= 5040	24 circles	= 8640
15 circles	= 5400	25 circles	= 9000
16 circles	= 5760		

turning points in the market. One can experiment with the computer to see which cycle has historically worked better than another. For instance, counting forward from a major bottom or top on the FTSE Index one can then anticipate the next turning point in the market. If we take the major low for the FTSE towards the end of September 1990, then using the divisons of the Gann circle (ie 90-day cycle, or even the 180 or 120-day cycle) we can identify the important turning points in the market.

Chart 7.2 highlights the 180-day cycle for the FTSE 100. It clearly illustrates that the top of the market and its turning point was in June 1991 and again in February 1992, just before the downturn that was to follow. The next major turning point in the market could be around 5 November 1992.

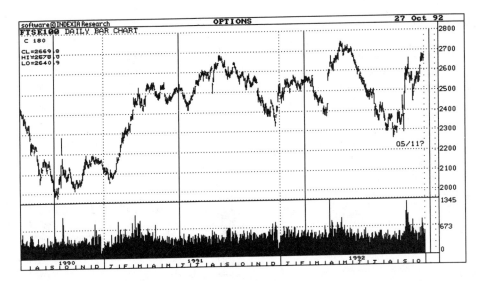

Chart 7.2 FTSE 100 daily bar chart, August 1990–October 1992
(180-day cycle)

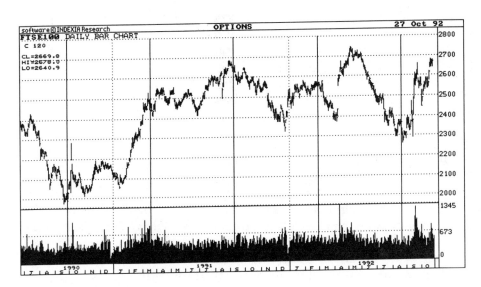

Chart 7.3 FTSE 100 daily bar chart, July 1990–October 1992 (120-day
cycle)

Chart 7.3 is a bar chart for the FTSE from July 1990 to October 1992. On
this occasion we have used the same major low in September 1990 but

have adopted a 120-day cycle. Again, important turning points were established. The first cycle highlighted the end of the bull run before a period of consolidation set in, while the next two cycles clearly picked the commencement of a new downturn in the market. Finally, the end of the down move from June 1992 was also highlighted by this 120-day cycle towards the end of August 1992. The end of January 1993 is the next important date.

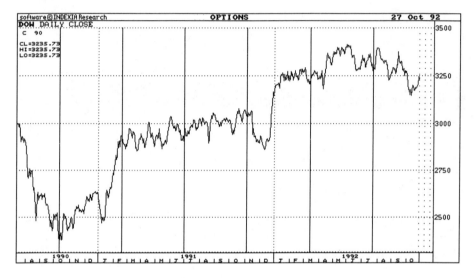

Chart 7.4   Dow Jones daily close, August 1990–October 1992 (90-day cycle)

Chart 7.4 for the Dow shows the closing price from August 1990 to October 1992 with a 90-day time cycle overlaid. Again you can see that from the major low in October 1990 the time cycle extrapolated from this point does in fact highlight a number of important turning points for the Dow. Even though the Dow has not trended very well over the last couple of years, turning points were picked up. For instance, in February 1991 the end of the recent bull run was highlighted and in November 1991 another important turning point was picked up by the time cycle.

GANN ANGLES AND PERCENTAGE RETRACEMENTS

Perhaps the most talked about technique that Gann used was his geometric angles. The basic concept behind these angles is that they are trend lines drawn from a prominent top or bottom, and the line is then drawn at a particular angle in relation to price and time.

The most important of these angles is the 45 degree and is known as the 1×1 angle because it is based on a one-to-one relationship between units of time and price. If one is drawing the line from a major high then it is drawn down to the right and vice versa from a major low. The understanding is that this 45 degree line acts as a major support level and in a bull run, as long as prices stay up above this 45 degrees of support, then the trend is still intact. Once the 45 degree line has been drawn then steeper lines such as 1×2 and 1×3 can be added in or, alternatively, flatter lines such as the 2×1, 3×1, etc. This simply means for a 2×1 line that prices are increasing at twice the rate of time.

Gann also used the 1×3 and 3×1 lines, but mainly with the longer-term weekly and monthly charts. The basic concept behind these lines is that once one has been breached then the price is likely to move to the next line where it may find resistance and fall back to the previous line which may now give it support. It is not quite as simple as this, and if you wish to have a more in depth understanding I suggest you read one of the many books available on W D Gann and his trading methods.

Once Gann had established the one-to-one ratio of time and price, he then calculated other ratios which resulted in other angles. Gann angles are determined by the ratio of time to price. Although the degrees are meaningless (because of different aspect ratios of charts), some analysts do however like to translate the Gann ratios into degrees. This is done using the arc tan of the ratio as follows:

- 1×8 = 82.87 degrees;
- 1×4 = 75.96 degrees;
- 1×3 = 71.56 degrees;
- 1×2 = 63.43 degrees;
- 1×1 = 45 degrees;
- 2×1 = 26.56 degrees;
- 3×1 = 18.43 degrees;
- 4×1 = 14 degrees; and
- 8×1 = 7.12 degrees.

Below the 45 degree up line is the 2×1, which indicates that one unit of price advances for two units of time and then the 3×1 and 4×1. The line above the 45 degree line in an uptrend would be the 1×2 which indicates an increase in two units of price for each unit of time, and then the 1×1, etc.

Chart 7.5 shows the daily bar chart for the FTSE 100 from October 1991 to October 1992. I have taken the high point at the end of May 1992 and one can clearly see the support line from the Gann angle all the way

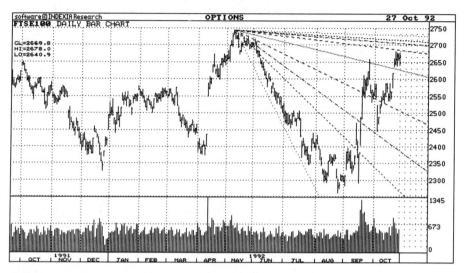

Chart 7.5   FTSE 100 daily bar chart and Gann angles, October 1991–
October 1992

down. Also, in the middle of September 1992, the −1×1 Gann angle
initially acted as a resistance level as the FTSE backed away from it.
Eventually, on its second attempt, it broke through and advanced to the
next Gann angle. However, on retracement, the −1×1 angle now acted as
a support level at the beginning of October 1992. Resistance is now
coming in at the higher Gann angles at 2660.

Chart 7.6 illustrates the hourly intra-daily close for the FTSE from the
middle of September 1992 to 27 October 1992. If we take the low point at
the beginning of October 1992 and extrapolate the Gann angles then you
can see that the 1×1 Gann angle has acted as a good support line.
Eventually a retracement may occur back towards the 2625–2630 level and
a bounce off from here would suggest further strength in the market. It
will also be interesting to see the percentage retracement levels for the
hourly chart.

Chart 7.7 shows the closing price for Allied Lyons from October 1991 to
October 1992. Here, I have taken the high point at the end of May and
again extrapolated the Gann angles. You can see how effective the −1×1
Gann angle was – all the way down this angle acted as a resistance line
until it was finally broken with a vengeance in the middle of September. It
then turned into a support line at the beginning of October.

Chart 7.8 shows the daily price for Sainsbury on a weekly basis from
1988 to 1992. In this instance I have taken the major low towards the end
of 1988 and the 1×1 angle has again worked amazingly well, although the

Chart 7.6   FTSE 100 hourly intra-daily close and Gann angles, September–October 1992

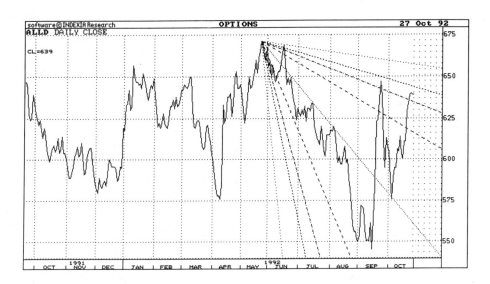

Chart 7.7   Allied Lyons daily close and Gann angles, October 1991–October 1992

Chart 7.8   Sainsbury daily close and Gann angles, 1988–October 1992

price did breach this angle to a certain extent towards the end of 1992. Quite often, analysts draw a parallel line to the 1×1 angle to further highlight the support level. In fact the overall uptrend was and still is intact, with perhaps a consolidation due back towards the 450–460p level.

Percentage retracements

Gann broke down percentage retracements of the price action into eighths ($\frac{1}{8}, \frac{2}{8}, \frac{3}{8}, \frac{4}{8}, \frac{5}{8}, \frac{6}{8}, \frac{7}{8}, \frac{8}{8}$) and also divided price movements into thirds ($\frac{1}{3}$ and $\frac{2}{3}$). As far as percentage levels are concerned, the 50 per cent ($\frac{4}{8}$), was considered to be the most important, followed by the 37.5 per cent ($\frac{3}{8}$) and the 62.5 per cent ($\frac{5}{8}$) retracement.

The technique was then used to combine both the geometric angles with the percentage retracement levels. By drawing the geometric angles from a major high or low and then using this major high with the major low to calculate the percentage retracement level, the analyst can build up an accurate picture of possible support and resistance levels. The analyst is looking for a pull back to the 50 per cent retracement level and at the same time an intersection with say the 1×1 Gann angle. Obviously, alternative combinations can be utilized.

Chart 7.9 is a bar chart for the FTSE 100 from November 1991 to March 1992. The high point has been taken from the beginning of November and the low point at the end of December. The percentage retracement levels are then automatically plotted and highlighted. It can clearly be seen that

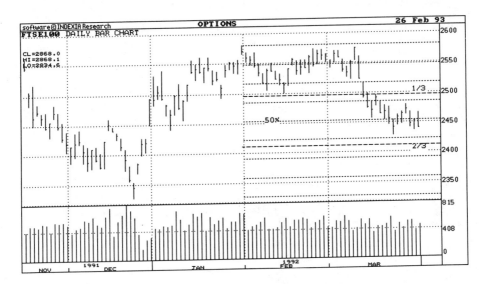

Chart 7.9   FTSE 100 daily bar chart and retracement levels, November 1991–March 1992

resistance occurred at the ⅓ retracement level, while the ⅔ level acted as a strong area of support.

   In Chart 7.10 I have highlighted the Gann angles together with the per-

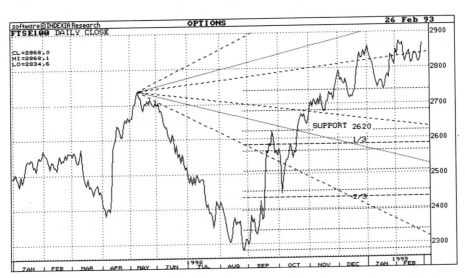

Chart 7.10   FTSE 100 daily close, Gann angles and retracement levels, January 1992–February 1993

centage retracements. Here we can see that the $^2/_3$ retracement level acted as resistance at the beginning of July and the $^8/_8$ retracement level (2383) acted as resistance in the middle of August.

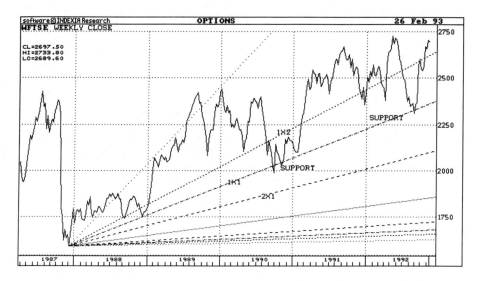

Chart 7.11   FTSE 100 weekly close, Gann angles and retracement levels, 1987–1992

Chart 7.11 shows the FTSE (weekly) from 1987–1992 and the 1×1 Gann angle has acted as a major support level throughout these years. Interestingly, when the market tried to rally in the middle of 1990, it found plenty of resistance when the price came into contact with the $^2/_3$ retracement level and the 1×2 Gann angle simultaneously, and it needed to have a pull back before again attempting to push through these levels. Similarly, strong support came in towards the end of 1992 when the 1×1 Gann angle acted as support as well as the percentage retracement line (the area highlighted on the chart as support).

Chart 7.12 shows the closing price for Kingfisher from January 1992 to February 1993. The Gann angles are drawn from the high point 'A' at the end of May 1992, with percentage retracement levels overlaid taking in the low point at 'B'. Support and resistance levels are highlighted and the reaction of the share price when these levels were hit can be seen. Resistance at 520p, support at 470p, etc.

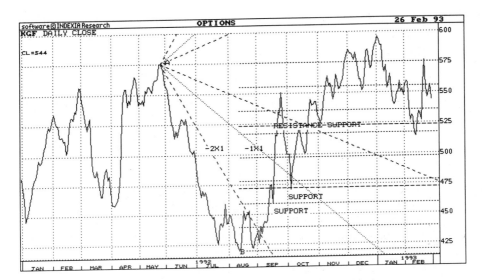

Chart 7.12 Kingfisher daily close, Gann angles and retracement levels, January 1992–February 1993

GANN's TRADING HINTS

1. Amount of capital to use: divide your capital into 10 parts and never risk more than one-tenth of your capital in one trade.
2. Always use stop-loss points. They should be mental stop-loss points. In other words, the stop limits are already placed in advance and you should remember these levels as the price approaches them. You should always protect your trades with stop-loss points three to five points away from the price paid (reference to futures market).
3. Never, under any circumstances, overtrade. This would be violating the rule on capital.
4. Never let a profit run into a loss. After you once have a profit of three points or more, continue to raise your stop-loss order so that you will have no loss on capital.
5. Do not buck the trend. Never buy or sell if you are not sure of the trend according to your charts.
6. When in doubt, get out, and do not get in when in doubt.
7. Trade only in active shares. Keep out of slow dead ones.
8. Never limit your orders or fix buying and selling prices. Trade at the market.
9. Don't close a trade without a good reason. Follow up with a stop-loss point to protect your profits.
10. Accumulate a surplus. After you have made a series of successful

trades, put some money into a surplus account to be used only in emergency.

11. Never purchase a share merely to obtain a dividend.
12. Never average a loss. This is one of the worst mistakes a trader can make.
13. Never get out of the market just because you have lost patience, or get into the market because you are tired of waiting.
14. Never cancel a stop-loss point after you have placed it at the time you made the trade.
15. Never buy just because the price of a share is too low.
16. Never sell short because the price of a share is too high.
17. Be careful about pyramiding at the wrong time. Wait until the share is active and has crossed resistance levels before buying more and until it has broken out of the congestion area before selling more.
18. Never hedge. If you are long of one share and it starts to go down, do not sell another share short to hedge it. Get out of the market, take your loss and wait for another opportunity.
19. Never change your position in the market without a good reason. When you make a trade, let it be for a good reason or according to a definite plan, then do not get out without a definite indication of a change in trend.
20. Stay with the trend.

8

Volume Spread Analysis

As previously mentioned throughout the book, I firmly believe that the correct interpetation of volume and its indicators should play an important role in the decision making for technical analysts.

The level of volume is a confirmatory signal of the rise or fall of the index/stock. By monitoring this, along with the price action, we are able to determine the buying/selling pressure associated with the market or stock price movements. As a market rises and the number of participants increases, the tendancy leans towards self-feeding price rises. Where there is a contraction in volume and price rises continue, this means that shares are being 'bid up' by market-makers, only with potential vulnerability ahead. The principles of volume trading are comparatively simple: Market strength is indicated (1) when the market goes up on heavy (increasing) volume and (2) when prices decline on light volume. Market weakness is indicated (1) when prices decline on heavy (increasing) volume and (2) when the market goes up on light volume.

Volume is studied by chartists since it is a measure of supply and demand for shares. It is the negative implications of the volume indicator that tells us most: that is, if volume is increasing sharply after prices have been rising for some time and then the price of the share stops or slows down, then the current supply has been met; or on the other side, if after a confirmed decline activity shows a definite decrease, the conclusion is that demand is being met. To summarize:

1. when volume increases during price declines = bearish;
2. when volume increases during price advances = bullish;
3. when volume decreases during price declines = bullish; and
4. when volume decreases during price advances = bearish.

Having briefly looked at the concept of volume analysis, I will now turn to a new program on the market called 'Volume Spread Analysis'. This program has been developed with the futures trader in mind and to date has produced astonishing results. The following sections describe the program in some detail together with supporting charts. However, if you wish to see the program in action and would like a demonstration then please write to me at Flat C, 6 Cromwell Crescent, London SW5 9QN.

THE TECHNIQUES AND THE PROGRAM

Volume Spread Analysis ('VSA') is not a new method. The techniques were first proposed by Richard D. Wyckoff in the early-1900s and have been improved upon since by numerous other analysts and chartists. The techniques seek to establish the cause of price moves and from the cause predict a directional effect on future prices. The cause is effectively the delicate imbalance between supply and demand in the market. The effect is often a large imbalance to one side or the other.

Over the years much has been added to the central core of VSA techniques, and surprisingly, it is these supplementary techniques which are more familiar to technical analysts than the main body of work. Well, perhaps it is not so surprising in these times because, as we shall see later, the techniques do not lend themselves easily to computerization.

Trend line and trend channel analysis, and point and figure charting, are the supplementary techniques. Trend lines and channel have been much maligned of late, and are largely ignored by modern technical analysts. Where they are used they are often misused, not drawn correctly and used to seek the wrong information. Point and figure charting is more widely used and appreciated.

It will be worthwhile to start by demonstrating the difference between VSA and other popular methods of implementing volume in other forms of analysis. Incidentally, I do not want to denigrate other techniques which have their place, and can be powerful in their own way. VSA is a complementary methodology, which adds to other systems rather than replacing them – be they technical or fundamental in nature.

Volume is fairly well understood, in broad terms, as the driving force behind price moves. Ask most analysts about the effect of volume and they will respond along the lines of 'Rallies and declines should be accompanied by expanding volume if they are to continue'. This is an intuitive response from the observation of many charts in which many moves are accompanied by expanding volume and terminate with shrinking, or climactic volume. This is a product of the eye's ability to recognize patterns. It sees what it expects to see and ignores the many moves that occur without the expected volume action.

The intuitive response is fine if you do not attempt to build an analysis system around it. If you build these principles into a mechanical system you will find that they fail as often as they work. The mechanical system is not fooled by an inate pattern recognition capability.

Price and volume

One failing of the majority of technical analysis tools is that they tend to separate volume and price action rather than combining the two. Most examine an area of a chart rather than a point on it. That is, averaging techniques are used to smooth what is seen as 'noisy' data. The net effect of smoothing is to diminish the importance of variation in the data flow, and to hide the relationship between volume and price action rather than highlighting it.

Accurately analyse the relationship between price and volume and you will discover that the *average* price can rise, fall and drift sideways on exactly the same *average* volume. There must obviously be other factors at work.

Modern volume analysis techniques are somewhat more reliable. The TRIN (Trading Index or Arms Index), developed by Richard Arms, is a finer tool. In this system a distinction is made between advancing and declining volume. However, having started to take a more appropriate approach, what do they do with it then? They smooth it.

Many analysts find equivolume charts (where volume is used for the x-axis of the chart rather than time) to be extremely useful. Here there is no smoothing at all and equivolume charts can be used to good effect if you understand the principles of the link between the volume, the price range and the underlying supply and demand. You can start by recognizing a fallacy in the volume/price relationship. This is the assumption that *high volume accompanied by a rising price is the result of increased demand.* Consider Chart 8.1.

With the advantage of 20:20 hindsight we can identify this as a technical rally following heavy selling, but using VSA techniques could we have identified this as such, before it came off, and distinguished it at this stage from a V market bottom? (A V bottom is where a major decline moves straight into a major advance, forming a major bottom in a V-shape without any obvious sign of accumulation.)

The market has been rising on expanding volume. In most systems this would be seen as a sign of strength in the rally. But note how the high volume up days are being followed by down days. This shows that the effort to drive up is meeting with resistance. Strong holders are selling into the rally, using the rising prices to liquidate their holdings because they are bearish (we cannot know their reasoning but we can see their selling, and if they are selling they are bearish).

The climax comes on the day under the cursor. Note that the day is gapped up, with high volume, and closes on it's high. This is the VSA view of what was happening. The market was in a technical rally after a protracted fall. There was sufficient buying to cause the rally, but for some

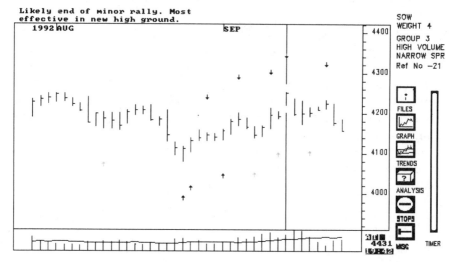

Chart 8.1   A short-lived technical rally following a severe decline

reason a significant number of professionals were feeling bearish enough to sell into the rallies. As the price gapped up through a resistance area to the left, buyers jumped in on the break out. Had there been enough of them buying we might have seen a continuation of the rally and the formation of a V bottom. The price spread (range) of the day would have been wide and up as market-makers raised their offers against the increasing demand, resulting in ever higher prices (see Chart 8.2). But here the spread has been narrowed as the market-makers (specialists in the US) filled large sell orders from the buy orders coming in.

The market-makers' perspective

Consider the position of the market-makers (or other floor traders in an open outcry system of market-making). The market-makers are in the unique position of being able to see both sides of the market as they are receiving a constant stream of buy and sell orders. Some orders will be filled immediately, some go, figuratively, 'on to the books' and will take longer to fill, and some orders will not be at the current price available, but at a specified price above (to sell) or below (to buy) the market.

The market-maker can see all of these. In the case above, the market-makers were carrying a large number of big sell orders. If you approached a market-maker with a bid he would offer you what appears to be a good price. He does this because the sell orders make him bearish in the short term, as he expects prices to fall. He is also in competition with other

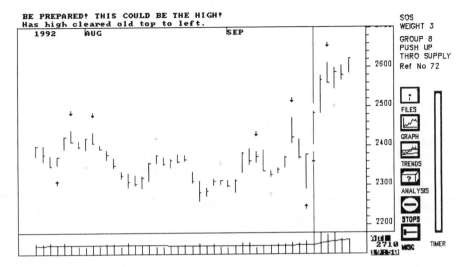

Chart 8.2   New high ground

market-makers, not only for your business, but for the business of a larger potential volume of selling. If a large number of trades take place under these conditions, the resultant narrowing of the bid/ask spread, narrows the price spread for the day.

So why don't prices fall under these conditions? Basically because the markets are liquid enough to absorb the greatly increased supply through the slight increase in demand, for a short time, without lowering prices. One acceptable definition of a liquid market, is one in which large positions can be taken without significantly affecting the price at the time of the transaction.

Here we can see the difference between the hammer and chisel approach of conventional volume analysis, and the diamond cutter approach of VSA techniques which seek to identify more subtle shifts in supply and demand. The beauty of this approach is that you do not need specialized information, just the high, low and close prices and reasonably accurate volumes. (Note that volume figures can be unreliable in some markets. But VSA is concerned with *relative volume* rather then the actual figures. Therefore, provided that inaccuracies are at least consistent, they are not too much of a worry.)

VSA techniques are subtle, but by no means infallible. The indicator described above (gapped-up high volume on a narrow spread) worked in the case shown and the rally ended. Had you been using the VSA program to highlight this indicator you would have seen that it was accompanied by a warning that the indicator was unreliable when not in new high ground, and could in fact be a sign of strength, not weakness. The advice issued was therefore to close up stop-loss orders tight, rather than to initiate a short position. (Had the indicator appeared in new high ground it would have been replaced by 'likely end of rising market' which is a sell signal.)

False break outs

Let's re-examine the logic in the light of the indication occuring with trading areas (especially an old top at the same level) to the left.

False break outs are commonplace. Many weak holders buy on break outs to recent highs, and then find themselves locked in to a losing position by a sharp reaction (fall in price). Rather than take the unrealised loss and cover the position, they hold out in the hope of selling on a subsequent rally (which is why they are weak holders). Some of these will hold a poor position through incredible losses, and some will make their position worse by trying to average the loss, taking an even larger loss-making position. These locked-in traders present a bit of a problem for professional traders on any subsequent rally. You can see evidence that this is so in virtually any chart when a rally approaches the area of an old top to the left. There is often gapping through this area or a very wide spread up beyond the old top. In VSA this shows up in a set of indicators called 'pushing up through supply'.

Strong holders who have accumulated most of their holdings at much lower prices will have to deal with weak holders, previously locked in to losing positions, who are now presented with the opportunity of closing their position for a smaller loss or even of breaking even. The professionals will not be keen to have to absorb selling at these levels as the supply hits the market because this action can reduce profits.

One manoeuvre to prevent this supply from hitting the market is to mark up prices rapidly through the danger zone. The weak holders, having at one time been faced with huge paper losses, suddenly find themselves in profit. A few may sell out, but for a majority hope is now supplanted by greed and they hold their positions. A good number will even add to their position. The amazing thing is that these people, having already been caught out once, will probably be locked in again later at even higher levels.

The sudden surge manoeuvre is not always possible to implement, however, and on occasion the supply from locked-in traders will have to be absorbed for prices to go still higher. In the previous 'end of rally' scenario, demand from weak buyers was overcome by supply from strong sellers. Consider the reverse scenario where the professionals are bullish and locked-in traders start selling into the rally. The market-makers are once more hit with a surge of sell orders, but this is a larger volume of smaller orders, mostly 'at the market'. If the strong holders are bullish they will be prepared to absorb this selling to maintain prices. The indication is exactly the same – high volume on a narrow spread – but now is a sign of strength, not weakness. In VSA techniques this is referred to as *absorption volume*.

Again, the subtlety of the techniques are highlighted, but so is the ambiguity for the unwary.

STRONG AND WEAK HOLDERS

The VSA program has over 150 of these indicators, though many are variations on a theme such as 'likely end of rally', 'likely end of rising market', 'pushing up through supply' and 'absorption volume'. All seek and highlight shifts in supply and demand.

These are the details of VSA techniques but the underlying philosophy is more fundamental and revolves around the interlay between strong and weak holders.

Most individual traders are either inherently weak holders because they have a weak capital base and an inability to carry temporary paper losses over a turn. Some with a broader capital base make themselves weak holders by their actions, mostly because they cannot stand taking losses and allow small losses to extend into big losses. They also fail to allow profits to run. But being a weak holder does not necessarily imply that you are a bad trader, just that you have a lower pain threshold than a strong holder.

Strong holders are the opposite – mostly professional individuals, or professionals working for corporate bodies with huge capital bases, and a consequently higher pain threshold.

The basic underlying premise of VSA philosophy is that a bull market starts when there has been a complete transfer of holdings from weak holders to strong holders, generally at a loss to the weak holders. A bear market will start when the transfer back from strong holders to weak holders has been completed, generally to the profit of the strong holders; then the cycle can begin once more.

Does this mean that a weak holder is never going to make money in the markets? Not necessarily, but it does explain why 90 per cent of non-professionals entering the markets lose money, and 90 per cent of new professionals fail to make money – which is not quite the same thing but has the same net result, failure. If the weak holder trades with the strong holders and not against them (ie, trades in harmony with the market rather than trying to beat it) the weak holder has the *potential* for *greater* returns than the strong holder.

How can that be? Well, it's not all disadvantage being a weak holder. Not by any means. But you have to play down your weaknesses and emphasize your strengths. One of the advantages of the weak holder is his/her small position size. Some other advantages are obvious, some less so.

Small and large-scale traders

Let's compare a small trader and a large one taking the same positions in a futures market. The small traders normally trade 1 to 10 contracts, the large trader 100 up to the limit. (Many futures markets have a regulated limit for the maximum number of contracts that may be bought or sold by one player.)

Both take a long position at the same price on a reaction into a low perceived risk trade. The smaller trader takes his maximum position in one hit, and execution is virtually instantaneous. The large trader has to scale-in to take a maximum position and his orders take time to fill, and even in the most liquid markets the price is going to move against him. You can pick up the phone say 'Buy 1000 at the market' but, except in exceptional circumstances, the order is going to take time to fill and the smaller trader is going to execute his position for a better price. He can dump his position if it goes against him, equally quickly. The large trader is going to have to make a more complex manoeuvre to exit from his position. This is an obvious edge. There are less obvious ones, which you can locate with extensive research.

On the OEX they have an electronic quote system (RAES) with a limit of ten contracts. The floor traders have obligated themselves to fill orders on this system at the offers quoted, *whether or not they can obtain those prices at the pit*. At busy times they might not be able to update quotes on the system for ten minutes or more. Hull Blair (quoted in *The New Market Wizards* by Jack Schwager) calls this the 'public's edge'.

The VSA trader tries to get an edge by behaving like the pilot fish swimming with a shark and picking off tidbits from the shark's meals while at the same time receiving protection from other predators through the shark's presence. This is the essence of VSA trading. Try to determine the consensus of professional opinion and go with the flow, not against it. It is essentially a trend-following system but one following trends in behaviour rather than in price.

ACCUMULATION, DISTRIBUTION AND CONGESTION

Accumulation, re-accumulation, distribution and redistribution during periods of congestion are well known, and form the basis of many and varied trading systems. Wyckoff urged his students to identify a cause for moves before taking on a position, and prior congestion is an obvious candidate for further investigation.

The point and figure (P&F) chart is a very useful tool both in the location and the analysis of congestion areas. The problems of trading accumulation and distribution areas is that you can never be certain whether congestion at the top of a move is distribution prior to a down move or re-accumulation for a further up move.

The VSA program creates an unusual P&F chart which incorporates *volume*. Volume is generally omitted in P&F charts because they are not time series based and have no time scale. Point and figure charting accumulates moves in the same direction, the charts consisting of alternate up and down bars. A reversal box size is chosen, and reversals smaller than this limit are ignored. Therefore if you are plotting an up series with a reversal box of 5 points and the price reverses by 2 points then advances by 6 points, the reversal is ignored and the up series is advanced by 4 points (6−2). If the price then reverses by 6 points (>5) the up bar is terminated and a down series starts. The net result is to accumulate significant advances and declines.

I do not want to get heavily involved in the analysis of congestion areas and trading the break outs because we have limited space and you could fill a book on this subject alone. I am more interested in demonstrating how the combination of VSA techniques and point and figure charts can help to solve the perplexing puzzle of V-tops and V-bottoms where the market moves from one phase to another without any apparent accumulation or distribution. This subject may also lead us back to the main flow of VSA and a phenomenon known as 'bag-holding'.

Chart 8.3 is a standard daily price chart of the FTSE 100 Index. Chart 8.4 is a P&F chart for the same period (10 point reversal). There is no obvious congestion area that might indicate accumulation in the bar chart, but in the P&F chart – hey presto! Chart 8.3 appears to disprove the theory that strong holders must accumulate holdings from weak holders before a sustained rally can take place. Chart 8.4, however, would appear to support the theory.

Taking a count from the P&F chart through the accumulation zone produces even more interesting results. This can be a bit of a pain with conventional P&F charts when done by hand, but the VSA program automates the procedure.

See how in Chart 8.4 we drew a line through the chart where the line could pass uninterrupted through the bars. The traditional method of taking a count involves simply counting the bars the line has passed through, but starting and ending with a down series (the darker bars). This produces a positive count (to get a negative count you would start

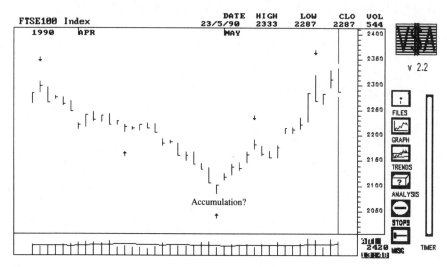

Chart 8.3   Bar charts and accumulation

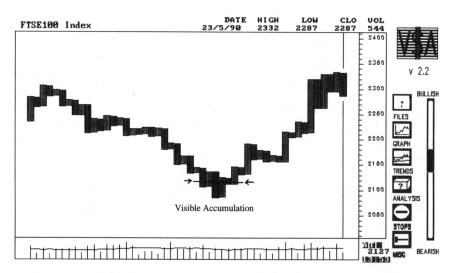

Chart 8.4   Point and figure charts and accumulation

and end with up series – VSA takes care of this automatically). The count is five bars. Multiply by the reversal box size and add to the close of the last bar to get your price objective – ie 5 × 10 + 2146 = 2196. VSA uses a slightly different automated procedure which produces the price objective shown on the chart at 2192. Note the level reached before re-accumulation on this chart – ie, 2192. Is it magic or logic?

Energy in a battery

Try looking at the market as a battery (also known as an accumulator). This particular battery is charged up during periods of relative inactivity. It then releases stored up energy to do work, say driving a motor. After a while the battery will run down and have to be recharged in order for it provide energy to do more work. *The battery can never release more energy than was stored in it to start with.*

It is often useful to apply a variation of this analogy to the markets and imagine accumulation as the storing of energy and the resultant up move as the result of the expenditure of that energy. Distribution can be regarded as the storing of energy to drive the market down. In this way we might see the market as a battery driving two motors, one for up moves and one for down moves. We might even extend the analogy to embrace strong holders as a positive charge and weak holders as a negative charge. Running the risk of taking an analogy into a flight of fancy, we might consider the effects of this storing and release of energy and the phenomenon of trend lines, which has never been adequately explained.

VSA has an automatic trending facility. Trend lines and channels have proven very reliable in warning when the market's battery is about to go flat. Price objectives from point and figure counts are rather like the charge indicator on a battery charger. They show us how much energy has been stored in the battery, but not how quickly the energy is being expended.

Correctly drawn trend lines are like an ammeter. The steepness of a trend illustrates the average rate of expenditure of energy. The price breaking up through the upper, or supply, line (in an up move) is a warning that the market is burning too quickly and a correction may be necessary (often to the lower or support line). When the price drops below this lower line it's like the lights dimming on a car showing the power supply fading. We can eke a little more life out of the battery by shutting down some systems and reducing consumption. A corrected shallower trend channel would reflect this. If there is no opportunity to recharge (through re-accumulation) the battery is going to go flat. Replace the battery with a capacitor (which has no limit to the rate at which it can be recharged) and we can apply the analogy to a bear-blowoff, where the accumulation occurs all in one hit – like a capacitor being struck by lightning. In VSA techniques we call this a selling climax. One peculiar form of selling climax is called bag-holding.

Chart 8.5 shows evidence of accumulation but not enough to explain

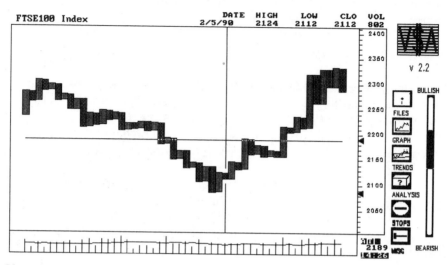

Chart 8.5

away the rally that followed, even allowing for the re-accumulation period shortly afterward. For an explanation of this move we have to turn to Chart 8.6 (and see also Chart 8.7).

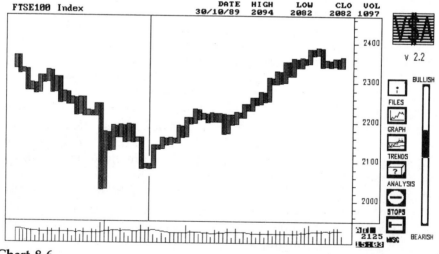

Chart 8.6

The market had been in a sustained bear move for some time following the long bull market of 1989 that everybody thought would go on forever.

A great many traders had been locked in at very much higher prices by the sharp down moves in September. They held out, in the main, because after the huge bull run, they expected the market to rally and get them out of trouble. By the time they realised that was not going to happen it was much too late to do anything but take the loss and get out. That very few did that is evidenced by subsequent events.

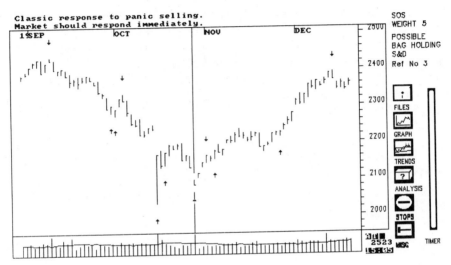

Chart 8.7

The market plunged to 2030 from a high of 2433 and many weak holders came out of the woodwork in a classic shake out on 16 October. Interestingly, some clung on tightly in the hope of better things to come. There followed a technical rally and promise of escaping with smaller losses which was cruelly snatched away as the market shot back into decline. Finally, the death blow to all hope came on 27 October when the Chancellor of the Exchequer resigned.

The open bag

The smart money had already taken their position during the earlier selling climax and, when the remaining weak holders finally abandoned ship, they almost literally held out their bags and let cheap stock fall into them. The action is very similar to the 'end of rising market' but reversed and exaggerated (it is easier to shake out on fear than to encourage foolish buying on greed).

The price gaps down into new low ground (you can ignore the shakeout spike) with ultra high volume on a narrow spread down. Had the professionals still been bearish the spread would have been wide and down as more and more desperate bids failed to attract offers. As it happened, strong holders were competing to buy this cheap stock as it hit the market, holding prices up and reducing the spread for the day. Less climactic action frequently occurs with lower volume and a close on the highs as buying overcomes selling toward the end of the day. Bag-holding, with very high volume and a close on the low, occurs maybe once in ten years, but is a classic buy signal. The close on the low may indicate that even furious buying could not absorb all of the frantic selling.

Cut and dried buy and sell signals do not occur all that often in VSA, and some clients were having trouble building a trading system around this charting system. As you are probably well aware, it's one thing knowing how to aim and shoot a gun, and quite another to blow a mugger's brains out with it.

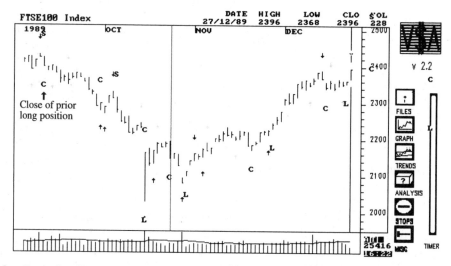

L = Long; S = Short
C = Close – price Close of short position; Below price cover long position

Chart 8.8   AutoTrade suggested trades

This caused us a bit of a problem at VSA Ltd where it is firmly believed that there is nothing more certain to guarantee failure than to impose your trading system on somebody else. It never ever works. The company needed something that could demonstrate how to trade the indicators but that was not so good that you could not outperform it with a little thought and intelligence. A program called AutoTrade almost succeeded – it

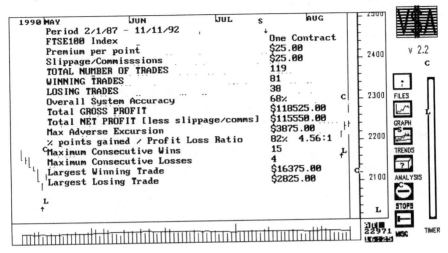

Chart 8.9   AutoTrade summary of results

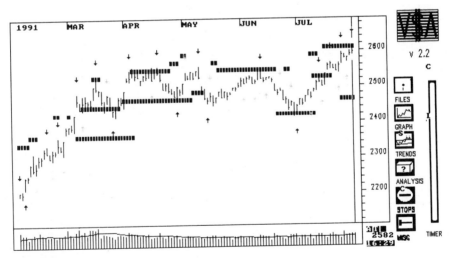

Chart 8.10   Trend line intersection

suggests entry and exit points using the same strategy as Market Monitor which keeps track of user initiated trades and calculates dynamic stop-loss orders to restrict losses and let profits run. I say almost succeeded because in some markets the thing is just too good. Fortunately it's not all that great at day trading, but just good enough to give you an idea of the right direction to take. An example showing suggested trades over the period just reviewed above is shown in Chart 8.8 with simulated results in Chart 8.9

VSA (the program) has 156 indicators at the last count, and as a leased product is continually updated and enhanced as the company encapsulates more knowledge into the expert system that drives it.

A final thought on VSA's unique approach to trading and analysis. Have you ever wondered what might happen if you stored every trend line ever drawn on your charts and extended them all to infinity? Apart that is from making a mess on your charts. What if you highlighted areas of the chart where three or more trend lines intersected. It might look something like Chart 8.10.

9

Japanese Candlesticks – Construction and Bullish Formations

Due to increasing interest over the last couple of years, I thought it would be appropriate to look in some detail at the techniques of trading the 'candlestick' formation. First, I propose to discuss the basic construction of the candlestick and then show with worked examples the formations that I personally have found most useful when trading the FTSE Index and the sterling/dollar rate.

CONSTRUCTION

The data required to draw a candlestick is as follows: open, high, low and close. The area between the open and the close is known as the *body* and forms the candle. If the market closes above its opening value, then the body is left empty (white) and is considered bullish. If the market closes below its opening value, then the body is coloured in black and is considered bearish (see Chart 9.1).

The highs and the lows of the days are then attached to the body acting as wicks (or often referred to as *shadows*). The shadows therefore represent the high (upper shadow) of the day and the low (lower shadow) of the day.

However, if the price closes on the high of its day (ie upper shadow) then the candlestick is said to have a *shaven head*, while with the reverse, if it closes on the low of the day, it is then called a *shaven bottom*.

In fact the same data is used to draw a bar chart as for the candlestick. But both are drawn differently and, in my opinion, the candlestick gives far superior information. As will be illustrated later, volume still has an important role to play and can be used in conjunction with the candlestick formation.

Charts 9.2 and 9.3 show the same data and period. The first illustrates a

CONSTRUCTION

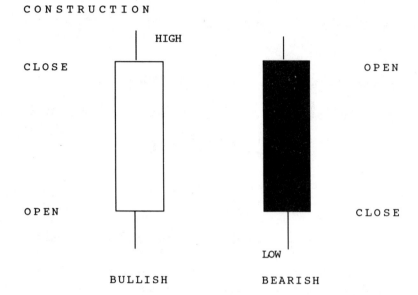

Chart 9.1   The candlestick formation

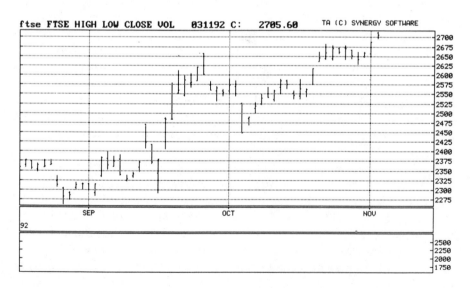

Chart 9.2   FTSE bar chart, August–November 1992

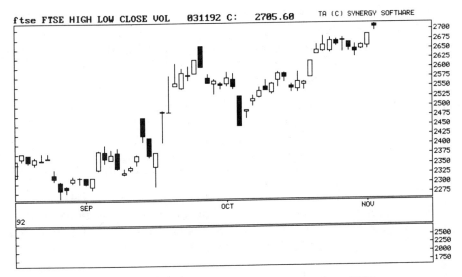

Chart 9.3 FTSE candlestick chart, August–November 1992

typical bar chart while the second is a candlestick chart. The bar chart clearly illustrates the high, low, open and close and this information together with the volume indicator gives the trader detailed feedback as to the mood of the market. However, just by glancing at the candlestick chart you can immediately see where the bears (black candles) and the bulls (White Candles) begin to take control, and by recognition of various candlestick patterns one can readily see possible trading opportunities. For instance, a *hammer* formation (bullish) appears after the downtrend in the middle of September and before the market took off!

I have found a number of candlestick formations of particular use and will endeavour to illustrate them with detailed worked examples.

REVERSAL PATTERNS

Hammer and inverted hammer

These are two of my favourite signals. Not only because they are very easy to identify but more importantly they do have a very high success rate. (By the way, don't forget you can still use candlestick charts in conjunction with your secondary oscillators and volume indicators.)

The hammer appears at market bottoms after a downtrend. The market opens and then falls away and forms a low of the day which is some way off its opening value (hence the long lower shadow) but it then rallies and closes near its opening value which consequently results in a small real body. The low of the day from the real body results in this long shadow, which should be at least twice as long as the real body itself. The Japanese word for this line is *takuri* which literally means 'trying to feel the depth of the water by feeling for its bottom'. In summary, the following criteria should be met for a hammer formation:

1. real body is at the upper end of the trading range;
2. the shadow should ideally be at least twice as long as the real body;
3. there should be no, or very little upper shadow;
4. occurs at market bottoms and after a downtrend; and
5. the signal is more bullish if the real body is white but a hammer can still have a black body.

The other point worth mentioning is that for the more cautious trader it may be prudent to wait for a confirmatory signal after the appearance of a hammer which would be a next day's white candle. (Even better if it is an *engulfing* white candle or the next's day's candle has gapped up.)

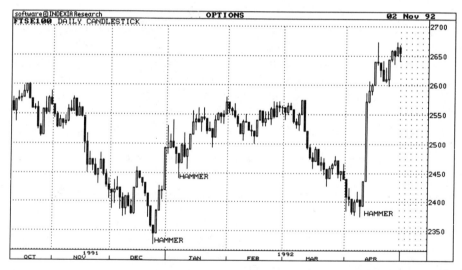

Chart 9.4   FTSE 100 daily candlestick, October 1991–April 1992

Chart 9.4 covers the period from October 1991 to April 1992. I have highlighted three clear hammer formations. First, one appears at the end of December after the downtrend from the middle of December. The next appears after the short-term downtrend at the beginning of January and, finally, a well-defined hammer formation appears just before the General Election. Interestingly, an *inverted hammer* also appears a day before the hammer formation in April.

An inverted hammer is another bullish formation and is exactly as described with the real body at the base, but with an upper shadow (twice as long as the real base) instead of a lower shadow. The important point to remember with the inverted hammer is that you must wait for a bullish confirmation before acting on it, and this was confirmed the day after the hammer formation.

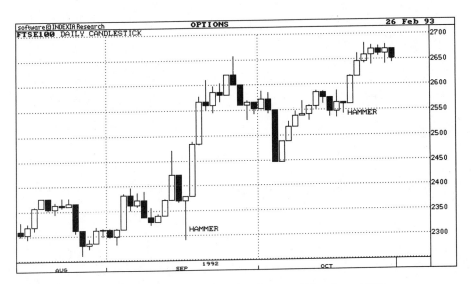

Chart 9.5   FTSE 100 daily candlestick, August–October 1992

Chart 9.5 again illustrates the candlestick formation for the FTSE 100 from August 1992 to October 1992. A further two hammer formations have been highlighted. Although there was not much of a downtrend before the hammer formation in September 1992, a bullish signal was confirmed by the white candlestick the day after and these two signals justfied the bullish sentiment.

Chart 9.6 shows two highlighted hammer formations. One appears just before 23 December 1991 and the second on 8 January 1992. Both occurred after a downtrend and both had lower shadows twice the length of their real bodies. The reverse of a hammer formation is a *hanging man*, but we will look at this formation in the next chapter.

Engulfing pattern

This pattern is both bullish and bearish. At this stage we will concentrate on the bullish engulfing pattern. This appears after a downtrend has been in existence and consists of one real body engulfing another (see Chart 9.7).

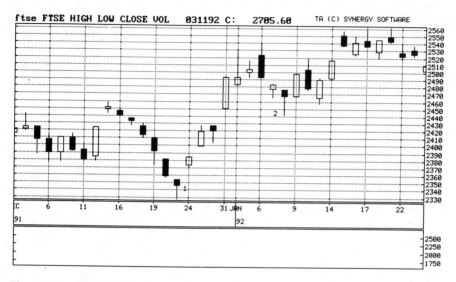

Chart 9.6   FTSE high, low, close and open, December 1991–January 1992

A   BULLISH   ENGULFING   PATTERN

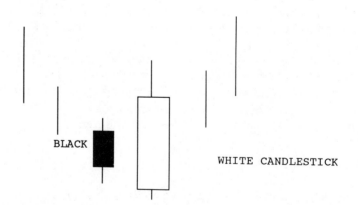

Chart 9.7   A bullish engulfing pattern

The engulfing white candlestick must be the opposite colour of the previous real body which, in this example, would be black.

The following criteria must apply: (1) the market must have been trading in a clear downtrend previous to the engulfing pattern; and (2) the real body of the engulfor must be in an opposite colour to the real body of the first candlestick. If the first real body is very small and the white candlestick (second body) is much larger, then this would be an even more bullish signal.

If the engulfing pattern happens after a short-term correction in the market rather than after a distinct downtrend, then cautious trading must be adhered to. In this instance it would be wise to wait for the next bullish signal which may be the very next day. Such signals could be another white candlestick which gaps up.

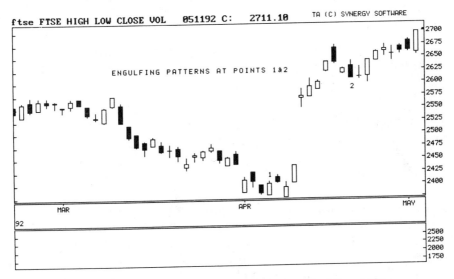

Chart 9.8   FTSE high, low, close and open, March–May 1992

Chart 9.8 shows a downtrend had been existence from the beginning of March and the engulfing pattern (1) highlighted on the chart occurred at the bottom of this downtrend at the beginning of April. I have also highlighted another engulfing pattern (2) where a short-term correction in the market had previously occurred but then an 'harami cross' appeared the very next day, followed by a white candlestick: these were confirmatory signals telling us that the market was now in a bullish mood, and sure enough it has climbed a further 100 points to date.

Chart 9.9 shows another engulfing pattern. However, the previous downtrend is not clearly in existence – rather just a short-term correction

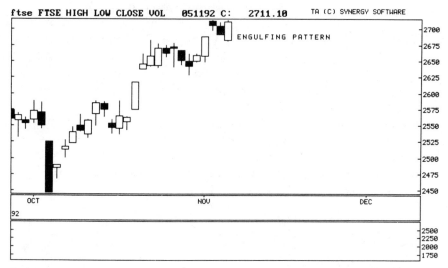

Chart 9.9   FTSE high, low, close and open, October–November 1992

at this stage. So before acting on this signal, it would be necessary to wait for a confirmatory signal over the next few days.

Piercing pattern

This is another bullish formation similar to the engulfing pattern. On this occasion the second real body opens below the low of the day of the first real body (black) – the lower the better – and commences to rally and closes above the mid-point of the previous black real body (see Chart 9.10.

The following criteria must apply:

1. Two candlesticks are required and the first real body is black and the second real body is white.
2. The second real body should ideally open below the low of the day of the first real body. However if it opens only below the close of the day of the previous real body then this should still be taken as a strong warning signal, awaiting a confirmatory signal the following day.
3. The second white body must penetrate (pierce) at least the mid-point of the first black real body.
4. The market is in a downtrend.

This piercing of the midway point is important and if in fact it fails to do

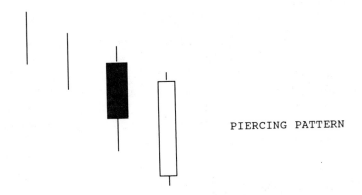

Chart 9.10 A piercing pattern

this and the next day is a bearish real body then it is highly likely that the downtrend will continue.

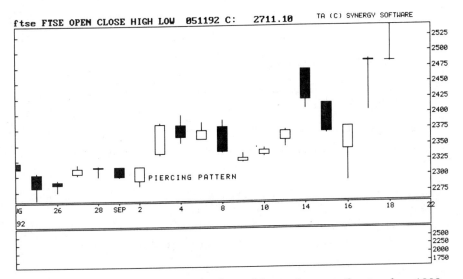

Chart 9.11 FTSE open, close, high and low, August–September 1992

Chart 9.11 shows a piercing pattern on 2 September which signalled a short-term uptrend over the next few days, although there were bearish indicators on the 14 and 15 September.

The hammer formation on 16 September, followed by a gap up, would have told you that the downtrend was now finally over.

Tweezer bottoms

This formation is not such a strong signal as the others, but is still worth noting. 'Tweezer bottoms' occur when the lows of the day of two candlesticks are the same. They can occur with shadows, real bodies or Dojis. They are called 'tweezers' simply because they look like a pair of tweezers. More importance can be attached to the tweezer formation if one of the real bodies forming the tweezer formation is itself a stronger signal, such as a hammer formation.

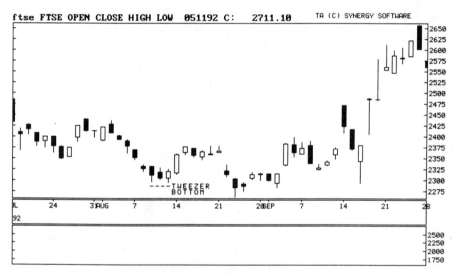

Chart 9.12   FTSE open, close, high and low, July–September 1992

Chart 9.12 shows a tweezer formation on 11 and 13 August where the lower shadows were both on the same lows.

In Chart 9.13 a tweezer formation can be clearly seen in the middle of October which led to the market's subsequent rally.

Stars

A star pattern occurs (see Chart 9.14) when a real body gaps away from a previous large body and then the third body moves well into the body of the first real body. Variation of stars occur when the first real body does not appear very large. It is not essential to have a gap between the star's real body and the third body, but if a gap does occur then the possibility of a trend reversal is stronger. Shadows can overlap and the important point

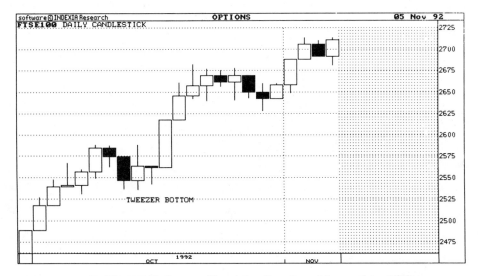

Chart 9.13 FTSE 100 daily candlestick, October–November 1992

to remember is that there must not be an overlap between the first real body and the star.

Morning stars occur after a downtrend, while their opposite, the evening star occurs at the top of the market in a congestion area or after an uptrend.

Chart 9.15 shows a clear morning star formation on 22 December 1991 when the previous black body appeared and then the market gapped down to produce a small real body – the morning star (colour does not have to be opposite). On the third day the market gapped up again with the close above the first real body's close. In fact this was a bullish formation on two accounts. First, the market had been in a downtrend and then the star appeared which also was a hammer formation. This rally was halted when a bearish engulfing pattern appeared at the beginning of January.

I have also highlighted variations of morning star patterns (1). These formations are not true morning stars because they were not preceded by a long black candlestick. Albeit the market did gap down from the first real body to produce a small real body and on the third day gapped up again to close above the first day's real body. On both occasions you should have been on your guard – at least that the temporary set back had come to an end.

Chart 9.16 covers the period from March to May 1992. At point A I have highlighted a Doji star.

A Doji star is preceded by a black real body and on the third day

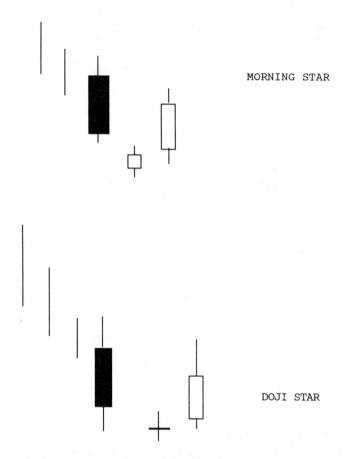

Chart 9.14   Morning and Doji star patterns

confirmation is required when the white body closes well into the first
day's black body. However, if on the third day, the market closes down
and below the Doji cross, then the downtrend is set to continue. It is
important to wait for the confirmatory signal of the white candle closing
well into the previous black's real body.

Point B highlights another variation of the morning star. On this
occasion there was a previous long black body and the market gapped
down to produce a small real body. But the next day there was again only
a small real body – although it did gap up, it closed just in the middle of
the previous black body. However, this can still be called a morning star.

The very next day an engulfing bullish pattern appeared. However, this
rally was short-lived and a warning signal was given when an evening
star (bearish) appeared the day after, coupled with a bearish belt hold.
(These bearish patterns will be discussed in the next chapter, but I

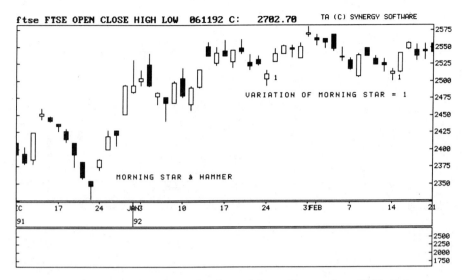

Chart 9.15   FTSE open, close, high and low, December 1991–February 1992

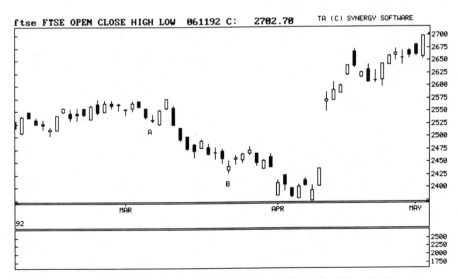

Chart 9.16   FTSE open, close, high and low, March–May 1992

thought it would be appropriate to mention them at this stage, so that you can begin to build up a picture as to the validity of the candlestick formations as a whole.)

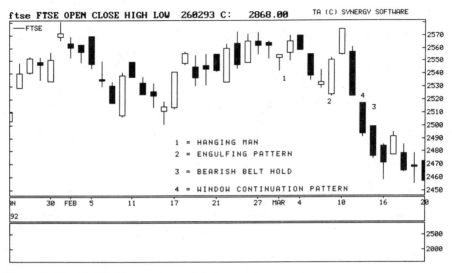

Chart 9.17   FTSE open, close, high and low, February–March 1992

Chart 9.17 highlights a Doji star at the beginning of March. Again this is a variation since the previous black real body was not particularly large and therefore less bearish. The market did gap up on the third day but again the rally was short-lived.

Another very important point to remember here is that one should always follow the trend – if the market is in a clear downtrend and a morning star or Doji star appears, then look at your other indicators to confirm the break out of the previous trend. I find it very useful to use my other indicators, such as the secondary oscillators and INDEXIA filters in conjunction with the candlestick formations to confirm a break out of the previous trend. For instance, if a previous hammer formation had appeared after a major downtrend, perhaps followed by an engulfing pattern, and my other indicators also confirm a major buy signal, then I would certainly be going long of the market with perhaps some longer-term out-of-the-money FTSE Index options on board as well as short-dated futures contracts.

Harami cross and Harami line

The word *Harami* in Japanese means 'contained within' and is simply a small candle body contained within the previous larger candle body (see Chart 9.18). If these Harami lines occur after a large market move then you should at least apply stop profits. Although Harami lines are used for highlighting possible reversal formations, in the main they are used for spotting short-term reversals within a major trend.

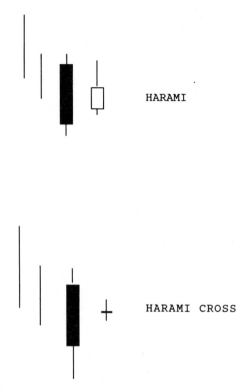

HARAMI

HARAMI CROSS

Chart 9.18   Harami line and cross

The Harami cross has the same opening and closing price (ie Doji) and if its real small body is contained within a previous large body, it is then referred to as an Harami cross. These have a greater degree of reliability in predicting reversal trends than the Harami lines.

Basically, the Harami pattern is the reverse of the engulfing pattern which we discussed earlier. The difference here is that the engulfing pattern's two real bodies are of different colours, but for the Harami patterns this is not important. Shadow sizes are also not important.

Chart 9.19 highlights the Harami cross at point 2 which clearly gave a strong warning signal that the end of the rising market was due; in fact this was further confirmed by the shooting star a couple of days later. The Harami cross was inside the previous white body and although there was initial upside a couple of days later, the correction downwards set in soon afterwards. As stated earlier, Haramis are useful in predicting corrections within a major trend rather than trend reversals.

Chart 9.20 shows Harami lines highlighted at points 1 and an Harami cross at point 2. The Harami line at the beginning of October was very

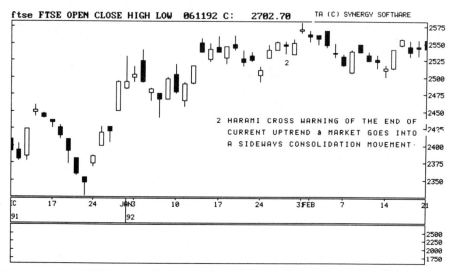

Chart 9.19 FTSE open, close, high and low, December 1991–February 1992

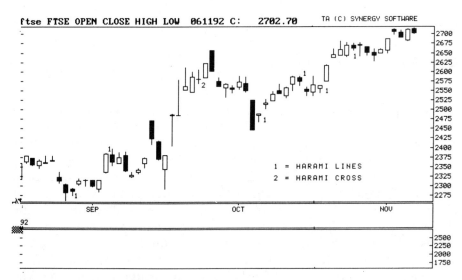

Chart 9.20 FTSE open, close, high and low, September–November 1992

bullish: not only is the previous black body very large but the Harami line was also a Hammer formation and, on the third day, the market gapped up. All in all a very bullish scenario!

CONTINUATION PATTERNS

Windows

A 'window' is simply a gap between the previous price extreme and the current price extreme. In other words, if a gap appears between the previous price's upper shadow and the next day's lower shadow (uptrend) then a window is formed, and vice versa in a downtrend. A point worth mentioning here is that support and resistance areas play an important role with windows. If, for instance, a window appears, the price subsequently pulls back and then closes the window, but instead of rallying from here, continues to fall, then the uptrend is no longer in place and the probability is that a new downtrend could exist, and vice versa in an uptrend.

The premise is that after a window has appeared prices tend to consolidate eventually and move back towards the window where they should find support if the move is to continue. If support is found at these levels, then the market will continue its move. In fact a move up from this support level is a good opportunity to go long of the market in an uptrend or short of the market in a downtrend.

As mentioned earlier in this chapter, it is always important to go with the trend and wait for confirmation from your other indicators as well before making a decision. If a window gaps up from a downtrend and an ensuing rally occurs, then before going long of the market – which at this stage would be bucking the trend – look for other confirmatory signals. It may be better to just cover your existing short positions.

In Chart 9.21 I have highlighted the windows in the uptrend and in the the downtrend. The downtrend that existed from June to September had three windows appearing when a technical rally ensued, and this was then followed by a further two windows in August. During the uptrend two windows appeared before a technical correction occurred, then a further four have appeared to date.

Interestingly, the number three plays an important part for Japanese technical analysts and on most occasions the third window that appears, whether in an uptrend or in a downtrend, usually heralds the end of that particular trend.

Chart 9.22 highlights the windows that appeared during the period from January to May 1992. Again notice the appearance of the third window in the middle of January before the market went into a period of consolidation. If we now look at the support and resistance levels during these periods and see how the market reacted as corrections in the price took place back towards the windows, did the trend continue or was it voided?

Chart 9.21   FTSE open, close, high and low, June–November 1992

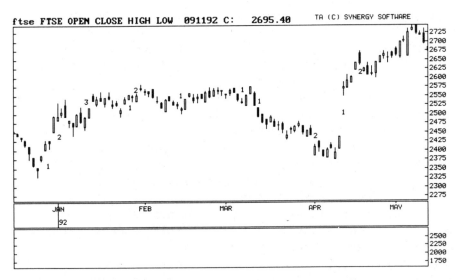

Chart 9.22   FTSE open, close, high and low, January–May 1992

Before leaving the window formation, there is one other variation of this pattern that I would like to mention. If during an uptrend a window is formed by a small black candlestick from a previous period of congestion, then this is indicative of further upside movement in the market. If on the following day the window acts as support level, during a correction, then the bullish trend will probably continue.

In fact this very scenario is happening in the market while I am writing this chapter (see Chart 9.21). The market gapped up on 3 November with a small black real body and the following day closed down on a correction but found support from the window. The next day an engulfing bullish pattern (white candlestick) developed which again confirmed that further strength in the market was likely and imminent. Then, on 6 and 9 November a bullish rising three method can be seen to be developing and will be confirmed if today's close is above the first day's close of the white candlestick on 5 November. Today the market opened down but is currently standing up 14 points at 2709.5. I believe there may be just a little strength left in the market – but beware – it is approaching a level of strong resistance and any bearish indicators could soon see the market falling off once again!

Three white soldiers

This is another continuation pattern. It is formed when three consecutive white candlesticks appear with higher closes and each white candlestick opens near to the close of the previous session's white real body. Also, the white candlesticks should close near their highs of the day. A rally is likely to ensue if this formation occurs near price bottoms or congestion areas. A

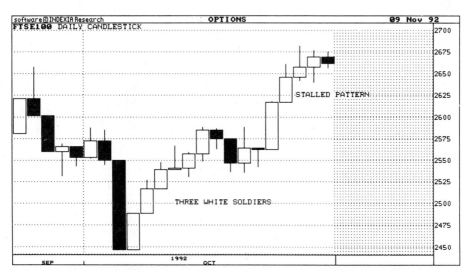

Chart 9.23   FTSE 100 daily candlestick, September–October 1992

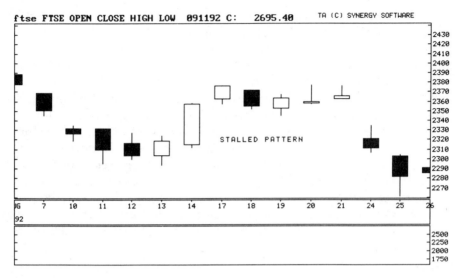

Chart 9.24   FTSE open, close, high and low, August 1992

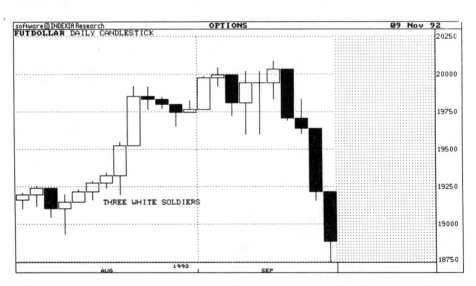

Chart 9.25   Sterling/dollar daily candlestick, August–September 1992

variation of the three white soldiers is the stalled pattern. Basically, this latter pattern means that the market is running out of steam and a period of congestion and indecision is likely to follow – normally this happens near market tops after a previous strong rally. A stalled pattern occurs when the last white candlestick's real body is small and preceded by a long white candlestick real body. Often the small white body also gaps up from the previous white candlestick's long body. Charts 9.23–9.25 highlight these patterns and are self-explanatory.

Rising three method

This is another bullish continuation pattern (see Chart 9.26) and is similar to the 'Flag' formation. It commences with a white long body and then profit taking sets in with the appearance of three (sometimes only two) smaller black real bodies which must hold within the previous long white candlestick. On the final day another long white candlestick appears, which should ideally open above the previous black real body and should close above the first day's close. One should also look at the volume indicator with this pattern. If volume is decreasing while profit taking is emerging, but then increases again on the last day, the uptrend is still in place.

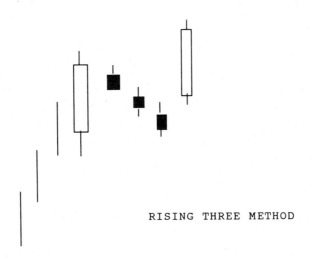

RISING THREE METHOD

Chart 9.26 The rising three method formation

Like with all candlestick variations, if in doubt then wait for confirmation from the next day. For instance, the last day may not close above the first day's close, but if the next day is a window which gaps above a resistance level then you know that the uptrend has been confirmed again. Also you can look at your secondary oscillators, Fibonacci support and resistance levels, fan formations as well as the Fibonacci retracement levels.

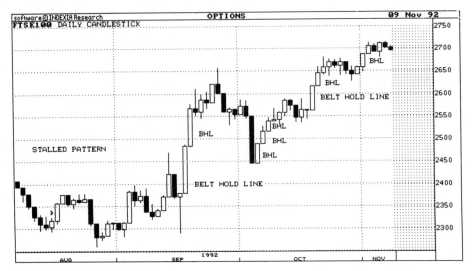

Chart 9.27   FTSE 100 daily candlestick, August–November 1992

Belt hold lines

Belt hold lines can either confirm a resumption of a trend (uptrend in this case) or signal a reversal of the previous trend. They do not give such a strong signal as the hammer engulfing pattern or the harami but are still worth noting. The belt hold line is simply a single candlestick and, if bullish, opens on the low of the day (or alternatively may have a very small lower shadow) and then continues to rally for the rest of the day. This pattern is also sometimes known as 'white opening shaven bottom'.

Another point worth noting is that the longer the real body of the belt hold then the more bullish is the signal that is being generated.

Chart 9.27 highlights the many belt hold lines (bullish) that occurred during the uptrend from September 1992.

10

Candlestick Formations – Bearish Signals

REVERSAL PATTERNS

Hanging man

The hanging man is the bearish equivalent of the hammer formation we discussed earlier. This formation occurs at market tops after an uptrend. It is called a hanging man simply because it fits that description!

The hanging man can have a white or black body but is more bearish with a black body. With the latter, the market opens at or near its high, then closes below its opening value and, during the day, prices drop off considerably to form the long lower shadow. The following criteria should be met for a hanging man:

1. real body is at the upper end of the trading range;
2. the lower shadow should ideally be twice the length of the real body;
3. there should be no, or very little upper shadow;
4. occurs at market tops or after an uptrend; and
5. the signal is more bearish if the real body is black.

Again like the hammer formation, the more cautious trader should wait for a confirmatory signal before acting on the signal generated by the hanging man. For instance a black body appearing after the hanging man or a 'dark cloud cover' (see below) would also confirm the bearish mood of the market.

Chart 10.1 depicts the candlestick formation for the IMM sterling/dollar rate for the period from June to July 1992. After the uptrend at the end of June a hanging man appeared which was a warning signal that this current rally in the market was about to end. Don't forget that in order for this pattern to be confirmed it should appear at tops of markets or at congestion areas. At least profits should have been locked in at this stage and with the next day's opening below the previous day's close then a

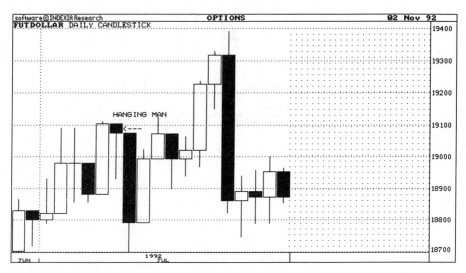

Chart 10.1 Sterling/dollar daily candlestick, June–July 1992

bearish mood was taking a hold on the market. The Doji cross that appeared three days before the hanging man formation was also a warning signal that the market was indecisive and that the uptrend was running out of steam.

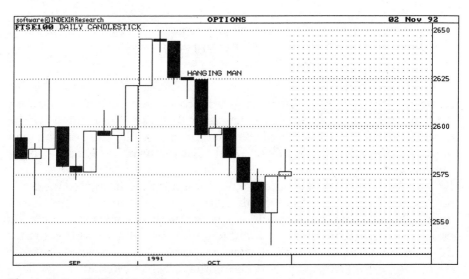

Chart 10.2 FTSE 100 daily candlestick, September–October 1991

Chart 10.2 shows a clear rally topping out at the end of September. Then, during the first week of October, a hanging man formation appeared followed by a bearish belt hold pattern, confirming that the current uptrend had come to an end. Previously, the Doji cross would have also put us on guard. This downtrend was finally over at the end of October when a variation of a bullish engulfing pattern occurred.

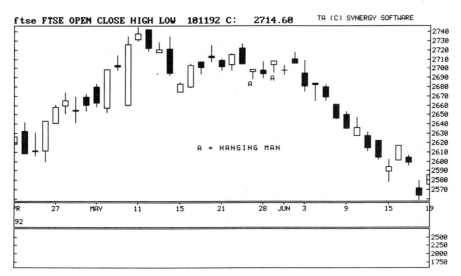

Chart 10.3 FTSE open, close, high and low, May–June 1992

In Chart 10.3 I have highlighted two hanging men formations that occurred at the end of May after the previous uptrend and during a period of consolidation. An Harami cross also appeared after the second hanging man formation, followed by a shooting star – a very bearish scenario – confirming that the bulls had lost the upper hand. At this stage my INDEXIA filters and the volume indicators were also confirming that the major uptrend was over and I also received a major sell signal at the end of May which proved to be very conclusive.

The hanging man formation is a very accurate warning signal that the previous uptrend is about to be terminated but, again, the more cautious trader can wait for the next day's confirmation. However, if as occurred with these charts, other bearish patterns are also appearing at the same time, then it is highly probable that a breakdown of the trend itself is about to take place.

As previously discussed, it is more important to wait for confirmation with the hanging man than its counterpart the hammer formation. The fact that the market opens near its high, falls off rapidly and then closes near its high, is in itself reasonably bullish. But if the market then opens lower the next day, those who bought long the previous day are left in a hanging position: these traders will soon close or cover their positions and this in turn often leads to a herd instinct with more sellers climbing aboard.

Bearish engulfing pattern

This occurs after an uptrend has been in existence and consists of one real body engulfing another (see Chart 10.4). It is the exact opposite to the bullish engulfing pattern discussed earlier.

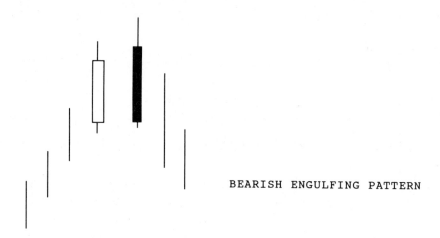

BEARISH ENGULFING PATTERN

Chart 10.4   Bearish engulfing pattern

The bearish engulfing pattern must be the opposite colour to the previous bullish white candlestick. The following criteria must apply: (1) the market must have been trading in a clear uptrend prior to the appearance of the engulfing pattern; and (2) the real body of the engulfor must be in an opposite colour to the real body of the first real body. If the first real body is very small and the black candlestick (second body) is much larger, then this would be an even more bearish signal.

If the bearish engulfing pattern happens after a short-term correction in the market rather than after a distinct uptrend, cautious trading should be adhered to. In this instance it would be wise to wait for the next bearish confirmatory signal.

Chart 10.5 highlights the candlestick uptrend from the middle of April 1992 to the top of the uptrend at the beginning of May. After a bullish white candlestick formation, a smaller upside white candlestick gapped

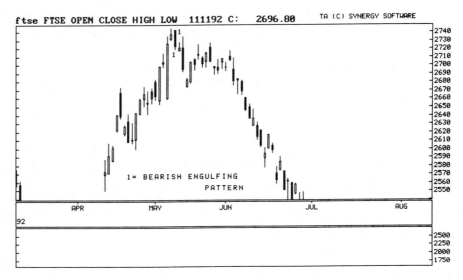

Chart 10.5   FTSE open, close, high and low, April–August 1992

up, suggesting further strength in the market. But this was immediately followed by a bearish engulfing pattern (1). The termination of the uptrend was certainly in jeopardy when the next two day's trading resulted in lower closes.

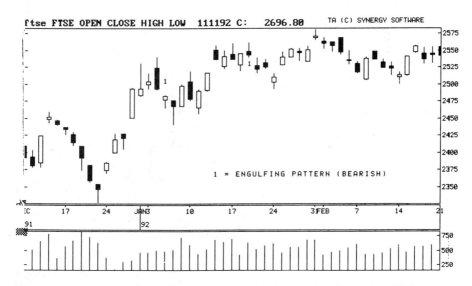

Chart 10.6   FTSE open, close, high and low, December 1991–February 1992

Chart 10.6 again highlights a clear uptrend from the end of December 1991. But again a bearish engulfing pattern develops at the beginning of January suggesting that this recent uptrend is coming to an end. Although an intermediate rally did ensue, the market finally entered a period of consolidation for the next month.

Tweezer top

This is the bearish equivalent of the tweezer bottom we discussed in the last chapter. Tweezer tops are reversal formations and occur at the top of market trends and are similar to a 'double top' in the Western world. They occur when there are two candlesticks with matching tops. The tops can be the real bodies themselves with shaven heads, or the upper shadows of the real bodies, or a real body and a Doji.

A tweezer top that comprises an Harami cross and a real body is usually a significant turning point in the market. Similarly a tweezer top with a hanging man formation would also be very bearish.

Again, it is wise to wait for a confirmatory signal after a tweezer top before going short of the market. However, after the occurrence of a tweezer top you should at least be looking at any open long positions and be tightening up your stop-profits at the same time.

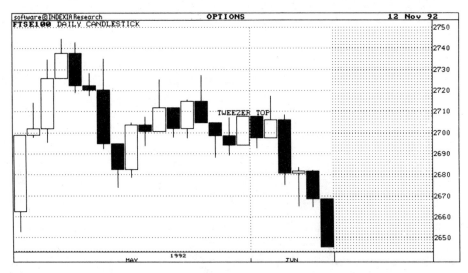

Chart 10.7   FTSE 100 daily candlestick, May–June 1992

Chart 10.7 shows the uptrend that took place from the middle of April 1992, with a correction and final period of consolidation at the end of May.

It was during this period of consolidation that a tweezer top appeared with two shaven head real bodies. The bearish engulfing pattern that occurred two days later in early June also confirmed the end of the uptrend and the onset of the downtrend. This, together with the hanging man formation three days after the tweezer top would also have signalled that the bears had taken control.

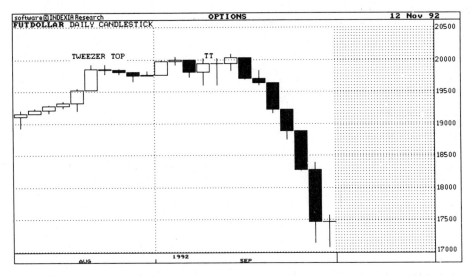

Chart 10.8 Sterling/dollar daily candlestick, August–September 1992

Chart 10.8 highlights the candlestick formation for the IMM sterling/ dollar for August and September 1992. After the uptrend from April to August 1992, sterling began to consolidate at the end of August and at this time a tweezer top formation appeared. It was made up of a white real body and its upper shadow together with a Doji. These two formations together were indicative that the uptrend had finished and the market was indecisive. A few days later another tweezer top appeared, made up of the same features. By this stage the uptrend had clearly finished and the market had entered into a plateau stage. Once the bearish signals started to appear (black real bodies and belt holds) it was certain that a new downtrend had commenced.

Chart 10.9 highlights four tweezer top formations and you can see that the market took corrective action soon afterwards. Mid-November could be another time for corrective action in the market. I would wait for the bearish confirmation signal, but we could easily see a correction to the 2700 support level. Incidentally, my Trend Setter program (see Chapter 5) has also confirmed weakness in the market and is now stating that we

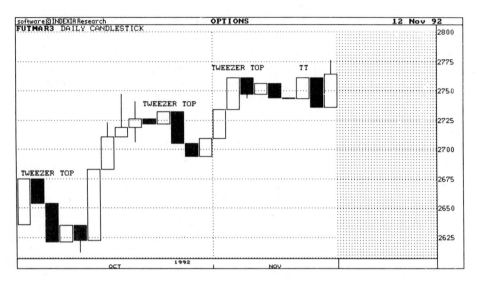

software ⓒ INDEXIA Research   OPTIONS   12 Nov 92
FUTMAR3 DAILY CANDLESTICK

Chart 10.9   FTSE March 1993 future daily candlestick, October–November 1992

should close out any open long positions; but as yet the program has not confirmed a major sell.

Dark cloud cover

This is a bearish candlestick pattern that occurs at the top of market uptrends or during consolidation periods after an uptrend. It consists (see Chart 10.10) of two real bodies – the first is a large white candlestick and the second is a black candlestick which gaps up on its opening from the previous day's close above the upper shadow of the first real body (white candlestick). It then proceeds to fall off and close near its low of the day. The important point is that the close of the black body should penetrate at least 50 per cent of the previous white candlestick. The greater the penetration, the more bearish the scenario. This pattern is the step before the engulfing pattern which engulfs the whole of the white body and is equivalent to the bullish piercing pattern.

Chart 10.11 highlights the clear uptrend from April to the beginning of May 1992. The first warning signal that this uptrend might be in jeopardy came when the engulfing pattern appeared at the beginning of May. Although an attempt at a rally occurred shortly afterwards, this soon flickered out and the appearance of the dark cloud cover, two hanging men and a star formation led to a very bearish scenario. Consequently the market soon entered into its long downtrend.

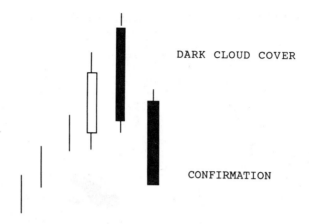

Chart 10.10 Dark cloud cover formation

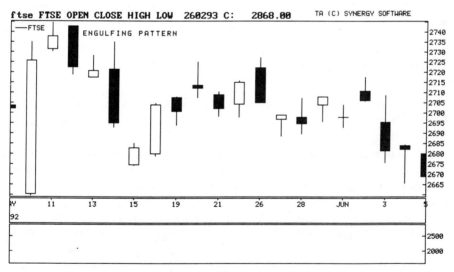

Chart 10.11 FTSE open, close, high and low, May–June 1992

Chart 10.12 again depicts an uptrend – this time from the beginning of September 1992. However, at the end of September a dark cloud cover formation appeared and the market took an immediate correction. Interestingly, volume was also falling away towards the end of this rally. The correction in the market was finally halted when an Harami hammer formation appeared at the beginning of October. Confirmation that a new uptrend was emerging was also given when the market gapped up the following day.

Chart 10.12   FTSE open, close, high and low, September–November 1992

Star formations

In the previous chapter we discussed the bullish star formations, such as the morning star. This time around we are looking at its equivalent bear – the evening star.

You will recall that a star formation comprises a small real body formed above or below an exhaustion gap. Ideally the candlestick preceding the star should be relatively large reflecting buying or selling blowoffs. The important point to remember here is that the real body of the star must not overlap the preceding body and the third real body must also ideally gap away and move into the body of the first real body, although this second gap is not as important as the first. Basically what the star formation is saying is that buyers and sellers are now in a position of stalemate and are not sure of market direction, and consequently there is an air of indecision.

Evening star

If a star formation appears after an uptrend then it is called an evening star. An evening star consists of three real bodies (see Chart 10.13). The first body is a large white candlestick which is then followed by a small real body which gaps up and away from the first real body. The third real black body can also gap away and down from the star but must move well into the body of the white candlestick. This formation is similar to the 'island top' reversal formation used in the Western world.

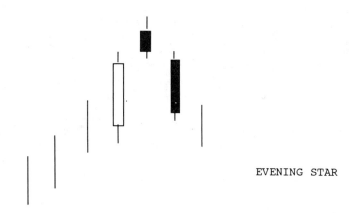

EVENING STAR

Chart 10.13   Evening star formation

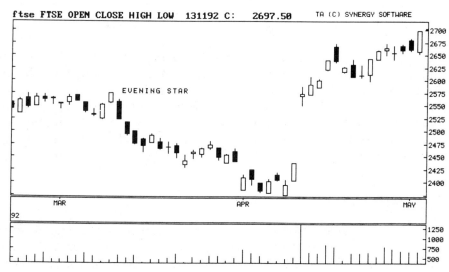

Chart 10.14   FTSE open, close, high and low, March–May 1992

Chart 10.14 highlights the candlestick formation for the FTSE. Before the downtrend commenced at the beginning of March, a clear warning signal was given that the bears were about to gain control of the market following the appearance of the evening star formation. The third real body moved well into the body of the first white candlestick and this, together with the clear upside gap of the star itself made it a strong bearish signal. Bearish confirmation was also received with the appearance of bearish belt hold formations preceded by an evening star.

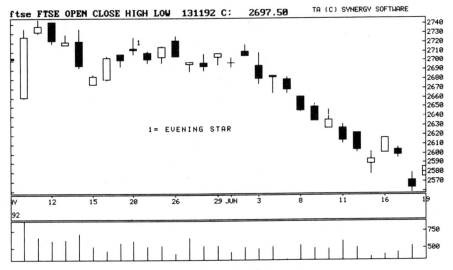

Chart 10.15   FTSE open, close, high and low, May–June 1992

A clear uptrend after the Conservative Party's victory in April 1992 turned into a period of consolidation during May (see Chart 10.15). It was during this consolidation phase that the bears started to get the upper hand in an indecisive market. On 20 May an evening star appeared, followed by a hanging man at the end of May, which in turn was followed by a shooting star at the beginning of June. This all led to a very bearish scenario and the rapid declines in the market between June and August 1992.

Shooting star

This is another trend reversal pattern but is not such a strong signal as the evening star. It appears at market tops after an uptrend and ideally it should also have a gap after the first real body. It is called a shooting star simply because it looks like one, with its small real body and a large upper shadow (see Chart 10.16). The colour of the candle is not of any real importance,although I still have more confidence in the signal if the candle is black which, by its nature, confirms that the market closed below its opening value. The shooting star is saying that the market had a strong intra-day rally that was finally rejected.

Chart 10.17 shows the top of the uptrend for the FTSE that started at the beginning of April 1992. I have marked a variation of the shooting star

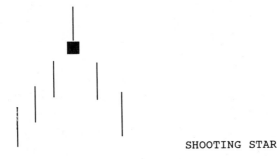

SHOOTING STAR

Chart 10.16   Shooting star

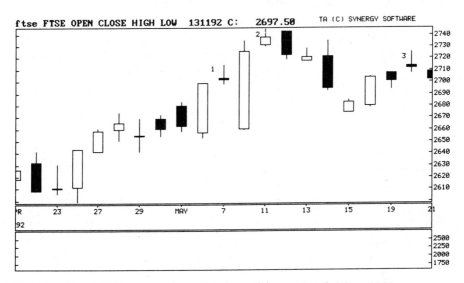

Chart 10.17   FTSE open, close, high and low, April–May 1992

formation at point 1, but this was not confirmed to be bearish because on the next day (8 May) a bullish engulfing pattern appeared and the first signal would therefore have been ignored. I personally always wait for confirmation of the pattern before taking any action in the market. However, at point 2 another shooting star pattern appeared and this was also a 'stalled' pattern which meant that the bullish sentiment had not followed through from the previous day (long white candlestick). Finally, on 12 May the shooting star was confirmed with a bearish belt hold. Point 3, as discussed earlier, was classified as an evening star but it could almost be classified as a Doji star which I will discuss in the next section.

As mentioned earlier, shooting stars do not have to gap up from the previous real body. However, when this variation does occur you must wait for confirmation and at the same time be warned that the current uptrend could be coming to an end.

Dojis

The Doji star is made up of a Doji cross combined with a star formation. A Doji is a candlestick formation where the opening and closing price have the same value. The Doji is perhaps the strongest signal of them all in predicting trend reversals.

Variations of the Doji cross occur when the opening and closing prices are so close as to still be able to call the pattern a Doji. By their very pattern, Dojis are areas of indecision in the market and for this reason they usually have a greater impact at market tops than at market bottoms.

Once the market top has been called and it goes into a strong reversal phase then the Doji plays a less important role because the market is often pulled down by the herd instinct during this downtrend. It is crucial to make a note of this: Dojis are important formations but are more reliable at market tops than at market bottoms and the latter should certainly have a confirmation pattern attached to it before any action is taken. Also, take little notice of Doji formations during downtrends.

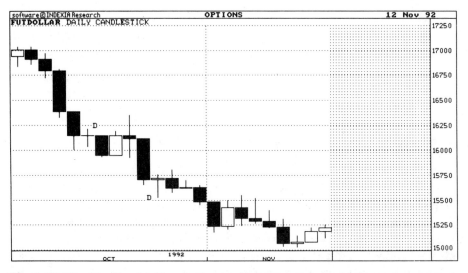

Chart 10.18   Sterling/dollar daily candlestick, October–November 1992

Before we look at Doji crosses in uptrends, Chart 10.18 for the sterling/ dollar rate illustrates the downtrend from October to November 1992 and

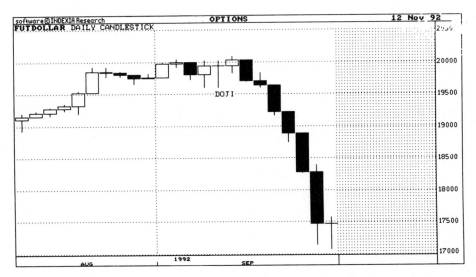

Chart 10.19   Sterling/dollar daily candlestick, August–September 1992

I have highlighted a number of Doji crosses (D) that had little effect in reversing the trend.

Although the Dojis had little effect during the downtrend, Chart 10.19 during August and September 1992 shows the sterling/dollar rate at the top of its uptrend with a Doji appearing just before the onset of the downtrend. This was definitely a warning signal and was soon followed by a bearish belt hold. There was no way you should have been long of sterling with these signals!

Other Doji patterns

Long-legged Doji

Again an important formation at market tops. As its description depicts, this formation has long upper and lower shadows. The market pushes higher during the day and, unable to hold on to this rise, pushes strongly lower (or vice versa) and then closes near its opening price. If the opening and closing of the long-legged Doji is at the centre then it is referred to as a 'rickshaw man'.

Chart 10.20 shows an uptrend in place during September; but all of a sudden a Doji cross (possible rickshaw man – 1) appears after two hanging men formations, themselves in the wake of a previous bearish belt hold formation and a rickshaw man (1) appearing between two white candlesticks. The market could not continue its uptrend after the

Chart 10.20   FTSE December 1992 future daily candlestick, September–November 1992

appearance of all these bearish formations and sure enough it suffered a hefty correction downwards until the beginning of October.

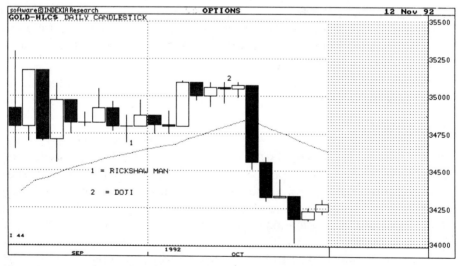

Chart 10.21   Gold daily candlestick, September–October 1992

Chart 10.21 shows the candlestick formation for gold. I have high-lighted a Doji formation at point 2 and a rickshaw man at point 1. Gold

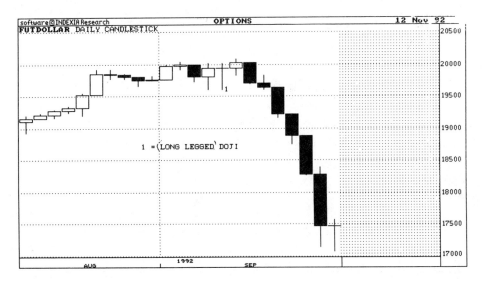

Chart 10.22   Sterling/dollar daily candlestick, August–September 1992

had been in an uptrend so we could take note of any Doji appearances. Although gold did attempt a rally at the beginning of October after the appearance of a rickshaw man it was short-lived and the market took on a very bearish scenario soon afterwards.

Doji formation for the sterling/dollar rate at the beginning of September is shown in Chart 10.22, before the downtrend and Black Wednesday!

Gravestone Doji

This is another bearish formation that appears at market tops. The gravestone is so called because it actually looks like a gravestone and is bearish. The open and close of the day are near the low of the day with an intervening rally during the day that fails to hold. The longer the upper shadow of the gravestone Doji, the more bearish the implications.

Chart 10.23 shows a typical gravestone Doji at point G in the middle of July 1992 after an uptrend. Gold then went into a period of consolidation before the downtrend commenced.

Evening Doji star

This appears when a Doji gaps above a real body and is followed by a black real body with a close well into the first real body (white candlestick). Again this formation appears during an uptrend or a consolidation phase after an uptrend. It is more significant than an evening star because of the presence of the Doji and usually signifies the top of the uptrend. Shadows can overlap for an evening Doji star formation, but if the shadows do not touch and there is a downside gap

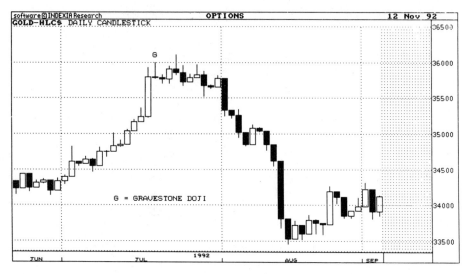

Chart 10.23   Gold daily candlestick, June–September 1992

on the third real body then the resulting (very rare) formation is called an 'abandoned baby' (see Chart 10.24).

Harami patterns

As a refresher, I will briefly explain what constitutes an Harami. It is the opposite of the engulfing pattern and the equivalent of an 'inside day' in the Western world. Harami patterns are not thought as significant in forecasting reversal of trends as the hanging man and engulfing pattern, but at the same time are worth noting, especially if a Doji is present to form an Harami cross (sometimes referred to as a petrifying pattern and very significant).

Put simply, an Harami is a small candle body contained within a larger candle body, with the smaller body forming after the larger one. The colour of the two real bodies is unimportant, as is the size of the shadows. I personally find Harami patterns useful in spotting short-term corrections in the market rather than trend reversals. However, as mentioned earlier, Harami crosses are more reliable (see Chart 10.25).

Chart 10.26 illustrates the end of an FTSE uptrend in January 1992 with an Harami pattern appearing on 29 January followed by a shooting star a couple of days later. However, action should not have been taken in the market until the day after the shooting star appeared when the bearish black real bodies gapped down. The short-term downtrend was finally halted on 10 February by the bullish engulfing pattern. Similarly a

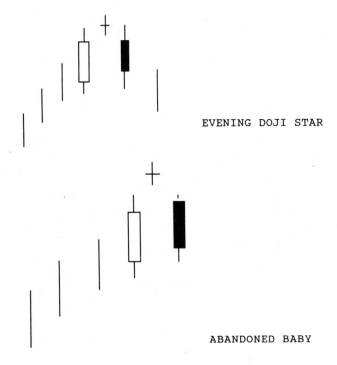

EVENING DOJI STAR

ABANDONED BABY

Chart 10.24   Evening Doji star

hanging man appeared at the end of February, followed by a bearish dark cloud cover at the beginning of March.

Upside gap two crows

This formation also develops during an uptrend. As the name indicates the two black candles appear after the market has gapped up. The first black real body gaps up while the second black body usually fills the gap, signalling a possible reversal in the trend. The first real body of the whole pattern is that of a white candlestick, usually larger than the two black crows. Ideally, the second of the two crows should open above the first one and then close under its close – that is, the previous black body's close (see Chart 10.27).

   The Bearish implications are that although the market is in an uptrend and has gapped up, it has failed to maintain its upside mometum and has in fact closed down on the day – but this close is still above the previous days close. On the following day the market obtains yet another new high but again fails to hold on to it and closes down on the day. But this time

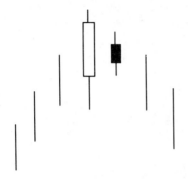

HARAMI IN AN UPTREND

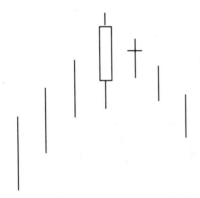

HARAMI CROSS

Chart 10.25   Harami patterns

the close is below that of the previous day – definitely with bearish implications.

Counter attack lines

These patterns are formed when opposite colours of the candlestick real bodies have the same or a similar close. A bearish counter attack line appears during an uptrend. The first candlestick is white, which is bullish, with a close above its opening value. The next black candlestick opens

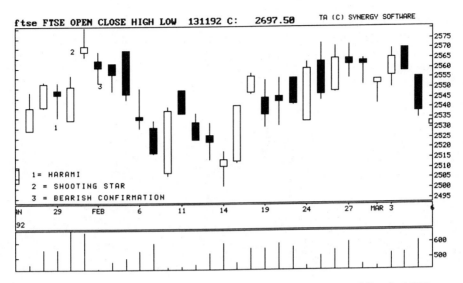

Chart 10.26   FTSE open, close, high and low, January–March 1992

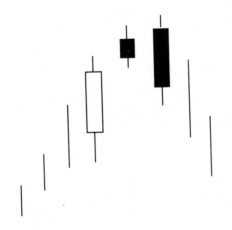

UPSIDE GAP TWO BLACK CROWS

Chart 10.27   Upside gap two black crows

higher but then closes lower (see Chart 10.28). In other words the bullish sentiment has run out of steam. This formation is similar to bearish dark cloud cover but on this occasion the black body does not close into the previous white real body and therefore is not as significant in predicting a trend reversal as the cloud cover and, in this instance, it is more important to wait for a confirmatory signal.

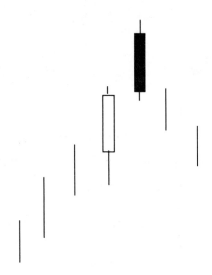

BEARISH COUNTER ATTACK LINE

Chart 10.28   Bearish counter attack line

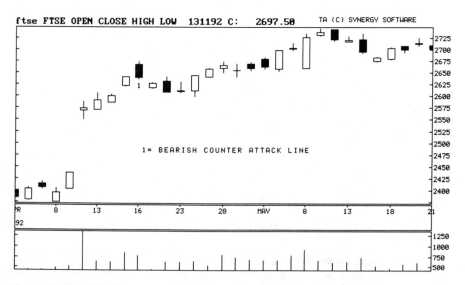

Chart 10.29   FTSE open, close, high and low, April–May 1992

Chart 10.29 illustrates the FTSE uptrend after the Conservative Party's victory. When the market became overbought, a correction rather than a trend reversal was suggested by the counter attack line at point 1. Also note that volume was not very heavy during this correction which would lend credence to the fact that there might be some steam left in the rally.

CONTINUATION PATTERNS

Windows in a downtrend

We discussed the concept of windows in Chapter 9. To recap, a window is simply a gap between the previous price extreme and the current price extreme. In other words, if a gap appears between the previous price's lower shadow (downtrend) and the next day's upper shadow, then a window is formed. As in an uptrend, support and resistance levels play an important part with window formations in a downtrend.

If a window appears but then the price closes the window and instead of pullback to recommence the downtrend the market continues upwards (after it has closed the window) then the downtrend is no longer in place and it is likely that a new uptrend could emerge.

The premise is that once prices have moved back to the window they should find resistance at these levels and then recommence the downtrend. A move away from these resistance levels is a good opportunity to go short of the market. It is important to stress that before trading a new position which initially could result in bucking the trend, you should look for confirmation of the new trend from your other indicators.

Chart 10.30 shows a clear downtrend in existence from 17 July 1992, then the market gaps down on 20 July. On 21 July the price moves up but closes down from its opening value (bearish), and it only just manages to close the window (possible resistance appearing). The next few days are also bearish (black real bodies) confirming that the downtrend is still in existence. Clearly this window acted as a strong resistance level at the end of July and the beginning of August.

You would not have gone long of this market until, at the very least, this resistance level had been penetrated on the upside and had been confirmed by a bullish candlestick pattern. As mentioned earlier, strong resistance appeared at the beginning of August and the renewal of the downtrend was confirmed by the dark cloud cover pattern on 4 August.

The window that appeared on 28th October during the downtrend (see Chart 10.31) acted as a strong resistance level over the next few week's trading. It was not until 20 October with the gap up by the bullish white

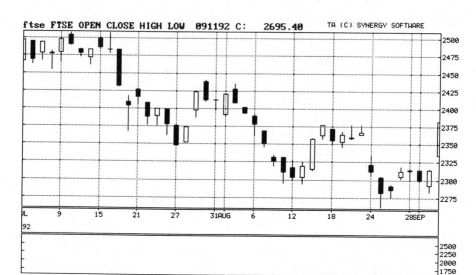

Chart 10.30 FTSE open, close, high and low, July–September 1992

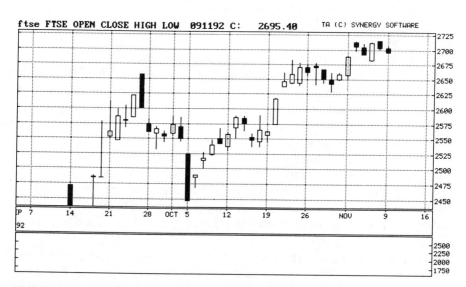

Chart 10.31 FTSE open, close, high and low, September–November 1992

belt hold above this resistance level that one could safely say that the downtrend was over.

Falling three method

This is the bearish equivalent to the rising three method we discussed in Chapter 9. In this case it commences with a black long real body and then profit taking sets in with the appearance of three (sometimes only two) smaller white bodies which must hold within the parameter of the previous long black candlestick. On the final day, another long black candlestick appears, which should ideally open below the previous white real body (but this is not essential) and should close below the first day's close of the first long black candlestick (see Chart 10.32). If volume is decreasing while profit taking is setting in, but then increases on the last day, the downtrend is still in place.

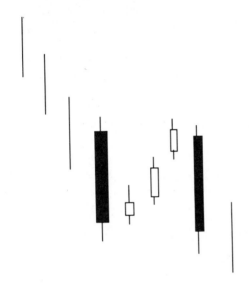

FALLING THREE METHODS

Chart 10.32   Falling three method

Chart 10.33 shows the clear downtrend in existence for gold during October and November 1992. However, at 33,750 towards the end of October the gold price attempts a rally and a variation of the falling three method appears. Ideally the last day should have closed below the first day. Nevertheless, the previous appearance of the hanging man and the Doji cross while the market was still in its major downtrend would have encouraged the conclusion that this rally was purely technical and further downward movement was likely to follow.

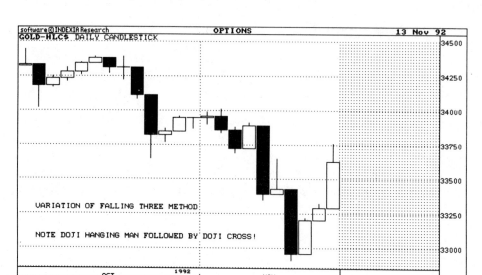

Chart 10.33   Gold daily candlestick, October–November 1992

Chart 10.34   FTSE 100 daily candlestick, May–August 1992

Belt hold lines

Belt hold lines can either confirm a resumption of a trend (a downtrend in this instance) or signal a reversal of the previous trend. They do not give such a strong signal as the hanging man, engulfing pattern or the Harami,

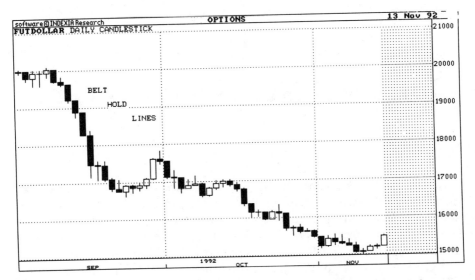

Chart 10.35 Sterling/dollar daily candlestick, September–November 1992

but are still worth noting. The belt hold line is simply a single candlestick and, if bearish, opens on the high of the day (or alternatively may have a very small upper shadow) and then continues to fall off for the rest of the day. The bearish belt hold is sometimes referred to as the 'opening shaven head'.

Charts 10.34 and 10.35 illustrate downtrend formations with the belt hold lines highlighted.

11

Options – New Developments

Perhaps the most recent change in the options market concerns the calculation of the margin requirement. The improved margining system is known as 'London Span' and was introduced by the London Clearing House (LCH) during 1991 for the following exchanges: the London International Financial Futures Exchange (LIFFE); the London Futures and Options Exchange (FOX); and the International Petroleum Exchange (IPE).

LCH is owned by six of the largest clearing banks (Barclays, Lloyds, Midland, National Westminster, The Royal Bank of Scotland and Standard Chartered). It is the independent guarantor and now clears both futures and options contracts for LIFFE and FOX as well as for the London Metal Exchange (LME) and IPE.

In order to cover its own risk exposure LCH requires initial margin on all net positions in the form of a deposit. This is only a guide and clearing members may impose a more stringent requirement if they so wish under the rules governing their relevant exchanges.

LONDON SPAN

This is the method used for calculating initial margin requirements. Basically it matches margin to risk exposure for a particular portfolio and is used for initial margin only, not for the calculation of any variation of the margin or for settlement of contracts.

Calculation

The calculation involves a simulated computerized program called 'Risk Arrays' supplied by LCH, which can then be simply loaded into a PC via a modem. Traders can then input their positions and the London Span margins are then calculated. (Further information can be obtained via the LCH Help Desk on 071–265–2127.)

As we already know, option values are affected by three criteria: futures

Table 11.1 London Span scenarios

Number	Futures price	Time to expiry of future price (range)	Volatility
1	Unchanged	–	Up
2	Unchanged	–	Down
3	Up	1/3*	Up
4	Up	1/3	Down
5	Down	1/3	Up
6	Down	1/3	Down
7	Up	2/3	Up
8	Up	2/3	Down
9	Down	2/3	Up
10	Down	2/3	Down
11	Up	3/3	Up
12	Up	3/3	Down
13	Down	3/3	Up
14	Down	3/3	Down

15 = Futures price up, extreme move (cover 35% of loss)
16 = Futures price down, extreme move (cover 35% of loss)

* ⅓ of time elapsed to expiry date

price; time left to expiry; and volatility. What London Span does is to construct 16 different scenarios to illustrate the profit or loss of a particular contract if these criteria were to vary. These 16 scenarios are the 'Risk Array' for the contract.The parameters are set by the LCH and may vary from time to time. The 'Futures Scanning Range' is the largest futures price move that the LCH requires for initial margin cover.

The 'Risk Arrays' are calculated centrally every day using the closing options and futures prices.

FTSE 100 CONSTITUENTS

Table 11.2 summarizes the FTSE 100 constitutents as at 2 October 1992.

Table 11.2 FTSE 100 constituents at 2 October 1992

	Security	EPIC code	Shares (000,000's)	Price	Market Cap. (000,000's)
1	Glaxo	GLXO	3,011	772.5	23,260.0
2	British Telecom	BT.A	6,173	355.5	21,945.0
3	Shell	SHEL	3,315	544.5	18,050.2
4	SmithKline Beecham	SB.A	1,359	931.5	12,443.2
5	B.A.T. Industries	BATS	1,480	826.5	12,232.2
6	British Petroleum	BP.	5,412	220.5	11,933.5
7	British Gas	GAS	4,310	243.5	10,494.8
8	Guinness	GUIN	2,002	521.0	10,430.4
9	HSBC Hlds.(75p)	HSBA	802	829.0	10,143.1
10	Hanson	HNSN	4,819	207.3	9,987.4
11	BTR	BTR	1,980	484.5	9,593.1
12	Marks & Spencer	MKS	2,749	330.0	9,071.7
13	Unilever	ULVR	808	1,077.0	8,702.2
14	Sainsbury (J)	SBRY	1,765	479.5	8,463.2
15	Wellcome	WCM	861	937.0	8,067.6
16	Grand Metropolitan	GMET	2,056	383.5	7,884.8
17	Imperial Chem. Inds.	ICI	714	1,098.5	7,843.3
18	GEC	GEC	2,712	252.5	6,847.8
19	Cable & Wireless	CW.	1,081	565.0	6,107.6
20	RTZ	RTZ	1,003	601.0	6,028.0
21	Natl. West. Bank	NWB	1,644	357.0	5,869.1
22	Lloyds Bank	LLOY	1,267	443.5	5,619.1
23	Barclays	BARC	1,604	348.0	5,581.9
24	Reuters	RTR	438	1,236.5	5,415.9
25	Allied-Lyons	ALLD	878	588.0	5,162.6
26	Prudential Corp.	PRU	1,875	265.5	4,978.1
27	Boots Co.	BOOT	1,036	470.0	4,869.2
28	Bass	BASS	864	537.0	4,639.7
29	Tesco	TSCO	1,947	221.5	4,312.6
30	Abbey National	ANL	1,311	312.5	4,096.9
31	Great Univsl. Stores	GUSA	247	1,530.0	3,779.1
32	Argyll Group	AYL	1,116	333.5	3,721.9
33	BAA	BAA	505	712.5	3,598.1
34	Rothmans Intl.	RINT	604	587.5	3,548.5
35	National Power	NPR	1,275	268.0	3,417.0
36	Vodafone	VOD	1,005	340.0	3,417.0
37	BOC Group	BOC	473	694.5	3,285.0
38	THORN EMI	THN	407	777.5	3,164.4
39	Cadbury Schweppes	CBRY	740	427.5	3,163.5
40	Reed International	REED	558	555.0	3,096.9
41	Kingfisher	KGF	497	500.0	2,485.0
42	Inchcape	INCH	513	467.5	2,398.3
43	Commercial Union	CUAC	446	535.5	2,388.3
44	Sun Alliance	SUN	802	295.5	2,369.9
45	Reckitt & Colman	RCOL	374	609.5	2,279.5
46	General Accident	GACC	436	509.5	2,221.4
47	PowerGen	PWG	781	281.5	2,198.5
48	British Airways	BAY	740	289.0	2,138.6
49	Scottish Power	SPWA	815	206.0	2,119.0

Table 11.2 continued

	Security	EPIC code	Shares (000,000's)	Price	Market Cap. (000,000's)
50	P. & O.	PO.	561	377.5	2,117.8
51	Land Securities	LAND	505	402.5	2,032.6
52	Pearson	PSON	546	355.5	1,941.0
53	Enterprise Oil	ETP	457	424.5	1,940.0
54	TSB Group	TSB	1,513	127.0	1,921.5
55	Whitbread	WHIT	450	421.5	1,896.8
56	Ladbroke Group	LADB	1,085	172.0	1,866.2
57	Courtaulds	CTLD	400	449.5	1,798.0
58	A.B. Foods	ABF	449	400.0	1,796.0
59	Bowater	BOWS	211	843.0	1,778.7
60	Rank Organisation	RNK	309	575.5	1,778.3
61	Thames Water	TW.	387	446.0	1,726.0
62	Redland	RDLD	479	358.0	1,714.8
63	Scottish & Newcastle	SCTN	416	412.0	1,713.9
64	Legal & General	LGEN	485	350.0	1,697.5
65	Rentokil Group	RTO	971	174.5	1,694.4
66	North West Water	NWW	357	449.5	1,604.7
67	United Biscuits	UBIS	495	314.5	1,556.8
68	Northern Foods	NFDS	569	270.0	1,536.3
69	Tomkins	TOMK	565	256.5	1,449.2
70	Smith & Nephew	SN.	1,009	143.0	1,442.9
71	Severn Trent	SVT	355	406.0	1,441.3
72	TI Group	TI.	473	297.5	1,407.2
73	NFC	NFC	553	251.5	1,390.8
74	Fisons	FISN	691	195.5	1,350.9
75	Bank Scotland	BSCT	1,150	117.0	1,345.5
76	Siebe	SEBE	388	340.5	1,321.1
77	Carlton Comms.	CCM	198	661.5	1,309.8
78	Guardian Royal Exch.	GARD	866	151.0	1,307.7
79	Arjo Wiggins Appltn.	AWA	810	160.0	1,296.0
80	Rolls-Royce	RR.	967	134.0	1,295.8
81	Anglian Water	AW.	295	432.0	1,274.4
82	British Steel	BS.	2,000	62.5	1,250.0
83	Royal Bk. Scotland	RBOS	781	159.5	1,245.7
84	Forte	FTE	819	151.5	1,240.8
85	Williams Hlds.	WLMS	472	262.5	1,239.0
86	De La Rue	DLAR	192	634.0	1,217.3
87	LASMO	LSMR	750	161.5	1,211.3
88	Tate & Lyle	TATE	355	335.0	1,189.3
89	Coats Viyella	CVY	576	202.5	1,166.4
90	Sears	SEAR	1,506	77.0	1,159.6
91	English China Clays	ECC	267	432.5	1,154.8
92	Smith W.H.	SMWH	271	426.0	1,154.5
93	Burmah Castrol	BMAH	183	627.0	1,147.4
94	Granada Group	GAA	424	258.5	1,096.0
95	Scottish Hydro-Elec.	SHYA	383	282.5	1,082.0
96	MB-Caradon	MBX	455	237.5	1,080.6
97	Southern Electric	SEL	270	391.0	1,055.7
98	Kwik Save	KWIK	154	665.5	1,024.9
99	Blue Circle Inds.	BCI	687	130.5	896.5
100	BET	BET	934	95.0	887.3

Index